Welcome

Kevin Winter/Getty Images

W hether you have picked up this publication because you are a die-hard Swiftie or someone who's curious to know what all the fuss is about, I hope you will find lots to interest you within these pages.

Throughout 2023 and 2024 Taylor Swift has been making headlines and breaking records, singing and performing her way around the world with her Eras Tour. The eye-popping numbers and fascinating effects of the tour on local businesses and global economies are collectively one aspect of the phenomenon she has created.

But when it comes down to it, what makes Taylor so popular with millions of people of all ages, flocking to her concerts, streaming her songs and buying her albums, is her relationship with her fans and the magic of her very personal music.

Her lyrics strike a chord with everyone who has ever had their heart broken or knows the excitement of a new romance. Her music spans so many genres, it's impossible to come up with one definition for her unique sound. Her stage shows are spectacular – massive and yet curiously intimate.

As a person, she is generous and open-hearted. She cares for her followers and loves her friends and family. She's a role model who is never caught behaving badly. She's charitable, supports fans in need, contributes to disaster relief and food banks and promotes musical education and singers starting out in their careers.

Put all together, she is hugely successful but also very much a normal human being, as I hope these chapters will reveal.

Sheena Harvey
Editor

Contents

Kevin Mazur/TAS23/Getty Images

Get Involved!

We'd love to hear your personal Taylor Swift stories (and any images you can supply) with the possibility of including them in a future special. Watch out for the Call Out Panels as you go through these pages and please use the email Subject lines indicated in each so your stories can be directed to the right team.*

*Content may be edited for style or length and the content of e-mails will not be published unless the sender includes their full name, postal address and age. All submissions from readers under the age of 16 years must also include contact details for their parent or guardian. Entries - including images - must be the original work of the creator and submitted by the creator or their parent/legal guardian. Contributions must only include content and images for which the sender is able to grant Key Publishing Ltd full rights for publication.
While we will try to include as many contributions as we can, we apologise to those readers who take the time to write in but don't get into print. Submission is acceptance of Key Publishing's terms and conditions which can be found at the following address https://www.keypublishing.com/contributors-guidelines/ . No payment will be offered.

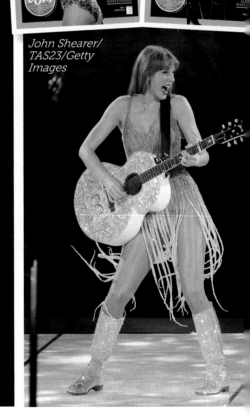

John Shearer/ TAS23/Getty Images

⌃ Ashok Kumar/TAS24/Getty Images
» Kara Durrette/Getty Images

ISBN: 978 1 80282 970 9
Editor: Sheena Harvey
Senior editor, specials: Roger Mortimer
Email: roger.mortimer@keypublishing.com
Cover Design: Lee Howson
Design: Key Publishing
Advertising Sales Manager: Sam Clark
Email: sam.clark@keypublishing.com
Tel: 01780 755131
Advertising Production: Becky Antoniades
Email: Rebecca.antoniades@keypublishing.com

Subscription/Mail Order
Key Publishing Ltd, PO Box 300, Stamford, Lincs, PE9 1NA
Tel: 01780 480404
Subscriptions email: subs@keypublishing.com
Mail Order email: orders@keypublishing.com
Website: www.keypublishing.com/shop

Publishing
Group CEO and Publisher: Adrian Cox

Published by
Key Publishing Ltd, PO Box 100, Stamford, Lincs, PE9 1XQ
Tel: 01780 755131
Website: www.keypublishing.com

Printing
Precision Colour Printing Ltd, Haldane, Halesfield 1, Telford, Shropshire. TF7 4QQ

Distribution
Seymour Distribution Ltd,
2 Poultry Avenue, London, EC1A 9PU
Enquiries Line: 02074 294000.

Taylor is a
Record
Breaker!

Big numbers and historic firsts are just part of the magic of Taylor Swift. To get you in the mood for our story of how she has wowed the world, here are just some of the records she has broken.

Kevin Mazur/Getty Images

Fearless made 20-year-old Taylor the youngest ever artist to win Album of the Year at the Grammy Awards, a record she held from 2010 until 2020 when 18-year-old Billie Eilish won the honour.

• She has won Album of the Year four times at the Grammys (*Fearless* in 2010, *1989* in 2016, *folklore* in 2021 and *Midnights* in 2024) beating Paul Simon, Stevie Wonder and Frank Sinatra with three wins each.

• The first woman to have 10 solo singles streamed more than a billion times each on Spotify.

• Musician who has won the most American Music Awards ever – 40 out of 49 nominations – smashing Michael Jackson's record of 24 wins.

• First recipient of *Billboard* magazine's Woman of the Decade Award in 2019.

• Spotify's most-streamed artist in a single day for *The Tortured Poets Department. All Too Well (10 Minute Version)* is the longest song ever to reach Number 1 on America's Hot 100, surpassing Don McLean's *American Pie* by two minutes and 16 seconds.

• Most Video of the Year wins at the MTV Video Music Awards – for *Bad Blood* in 2015, *You Need to Calm Down* in 2019, *All Too Well: The Short Film* in 2022 and *Anti-Hero* in 2023.

• First musician to be a billionaire solely from the sales of her music and stage performances.

• The Eras Tour is the highest-grossing concert tour in history, set to be around $2 billion by the end, against Elton John's record of $939 million generated by his farewell tour in 2023.

• Highest number of weeks in the top 10 of *Billboard* magazine's 200 chart. Her 10 albums spent a combined 384 weeks up there; the previous record was 382 weeks for The Beatles with 32 albums.

• A record 2.4 million concert tickets sold in a single day for the Eras Tour.

• First woman to appear on *Time* magazine's cover as Person of the Year twice – in 2023 as a single recipient and in 2017 as a part of a group inspiring women to "stop accepting unacceptable" conduct.

A Star is Born

Here's a timeline of some of the most important dates in Tay Tay's career.

Larry Busacca/ACM2015/ Getty Images

1997

Family move to Wyomissing and Taylor goes to Junior High School and commutes to New York for vocal and acting lessons.

2001

Andrea takes Taylor to Nashville to hand out demo tapes of Dixie Chicks covers, but no one is interested.

2002

Taylor learns the guitar and begins song writing.

2003

Performs original songs for RCA Records, gets an artist development deal, and begins weekly coaching sessions with country songwriter Liz Rose.

1989

Born on December 13 in West Reading, Pennsylvania to Scott and Andrea Swift who name her after the music legend James Taylor.

2004

Family relocates to Hendersonville, Tennessee, near Nashville and at 14 she becomes the youngest ever signing by Sony/ATV Tree.

Wyomissing high school.
Amy Lutz/dreamstime.com

Kevin Mazur/WireImage

Jason Kempin/
Getty Images

S_bukley/
dreamstime.com

Jeff Kravitz/FilmMagic

2005

Spotted singing in Nashville's Bluebird Café and signed by Scott Borchetta who is about to launch Big Machine Records.

2006

First album, *Taylor Swift,* is released and spends 157 weeks in the *Billboard* magazine charts.

2008

Fearless album is released, she dates Joe Jonas (top right) of The Jonas Brothers, wins Top New Female Vocalist at the Country Music Awards, and embarks on her first concert tour.

2009

Fearless becomes US best-selling album of the year and she hooks up with Taylor Lautner while filming *Valentine's Day* to become 'Taylor Squared'.

Acceptance speech for Best Female Vocal at the MTV Video Music Awards (above right) is interrupted by rapper Kanye West promoting Beyoncé's *Single Ladies*.

The big year continues with four Grammy Awards, Country Music Association Awards' Album of the Year, and an acting debut in a *CSI: Crime Scene Investigation* episode.

2010

Speak Now drops and sells over a million copies in the first week; a brief, painful fling with singer John Mayer is followed by a short time with actor Jake Gyllenhaal.

2011

Speak Now World Tour covers 13 months, four continents and 110 shows; Taylor's parents split but remain friends.

Taylor receives the Nashville Symphony's prestigious Harmony Award, recognising her for exemplifying the unique harmony between the many worlds of music that exist in Nashville.

2012

Another short relationship, this time with politician's son Conor Kennedy, and a longer romance with UK singer Harry Styles.

Red is released and becomes her first number one album in the UK.

2013

The *Red* Tour hits the world, is seen by 1.7 million people and enters the record books as the highest grossing tour by a country artist.

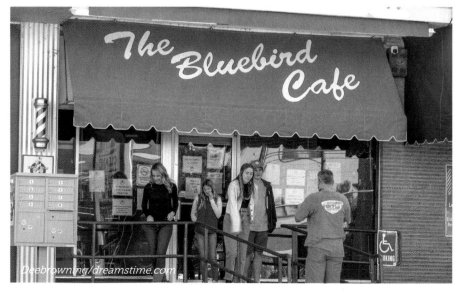
The Bluebird Cafe
Deebrowning/dreamstime.com

Moving Away from Country

Liam Goodner/shutterstock

Amnesia Ibiza/
Wikimedia
Commons

Paolo V/
Wikimedia
Commons

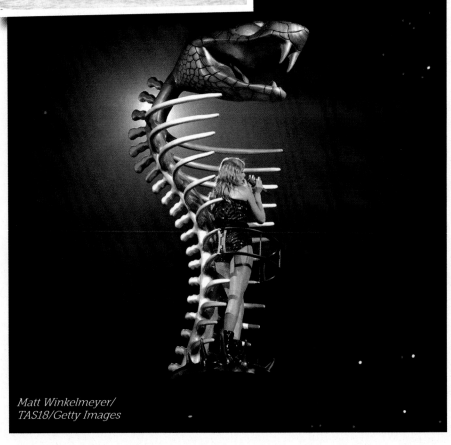

Matt Winkelmeyer/
TAS18/Getty Images

2014

A move to live in New York city, the recording of *1989*, which immediately tops *Billboard* magazine's Top 200, as well as a role in *The Giver* sci-fi film.

Apart from one song, Taylor's music catalogue is removed from Spotify and other free streaming services amid discussions about artists' royalty payments.

2015

After many months without a partner, Taylor teams up with DJ Calvin Harris (above) and wins an Album of the Year Grammy for the second time. The *1989* tour takes up the second half of the year.

2016

Kanye West writes a song claiming he made Taylor famous, and the ensuing social media storm leads to her being 'cancelled' by many online.

After a brief fling with actor Tom Hiddleston, Taylor begins a six-year relationship with Joe Alwyn and moves out of the public eye.

2017

Reputation arrives and tops the US, UK, Canada, and Australia album charts; Taylor's music returns to Spotify.

Octavio Jones/ TAS23/Getty Images

2021

Fearless (Taylor's Version) becomes the first re-recorded album to chart *Billboard* magazine's Top 200.

2022

The *Midnights* album drops and tops the charts in at least 14 countries. Taylor wins multiple trophies at the American Music Awards.

2023

Taylor is the year's most streamed artist on Spotify, Amazon Music, and Apple Music and has five of the ten best-selling albums in the same 12 months.

The Eras Tour begins and becomes the highest-grossing concert tour in history. Taylor's relationship with football star Travis Kelce (below) kicks off.

2018

Taylor beats Whitney Houston's record for most American Music Awards, having 23 in total, the *Reputation* stadium tour begins, and she signs with Universal Music Group (UMG).

2019

Lover, the first album on UMG's Republic Records comes out and tops charts in UK, US, Canada, Australia, Norway, Sweden, Mexico, and Ireland.

Record executive Scooter Braun buys Big Machine records and gets the rights to the recordings of Taylor's first six albums, which he then sells to Shamrock Holdings.

2020

The COVID-19 pandemic strikes, documentary *Miss Americana* comes out, and Taylor begins re-recording her back catalogue as *Taylor's Version,* with rewrites and extra tracks.

Lockdown albums *folklore* and *evermore* are released, Taylor becomes the highest paid solo musician in the world and plays Bombalurina in the movie of *Cats.*

Paolo Villanueva/ Wikimedia Commons

2024

The Tortured Poets Department album gets a surprise release, along with *The Anthology* edition, which makes it a double album with its 15 extra tracks.

The Eras Tour breaks all records for concerts and attendances.

Ezra Shaw/Getty Images

The Early Years

IN PENNSYLVANIA

Growing up was a mixed experience for Taylor, with loving and supportive parents but limited popularity at school. Both fed into the person she was to become.

☆ **An aerial view of Stone Harbor, where Taylor's family had a holiday home and she sang at a local coffee shop. The large building is the Villa Maria by the Sea Catholic retreat house.** *Carol M Highsmith Archive, Library of Congress/picryl.com*

Taylor Alison Swift was born on December 13, 1989 in West Reading in Pennsylvania, a settlement that grew from a single brick house in 1810 to the small town of around 4,000 inhabitants it is today. In the 19th and early 20th century the town was known for manufacturing hats and undergarments and is now home to a manufacturer of seasonal novelty chocolates.

Despite its commercial side, the area is also artistic and on Cherry Street, leading towards the adjacent town of Wyomissing, there are dozens of street art murals, including one of Taylor. In fact, quite a few murals of our favourite singer/songwriter have been decorating buildings around the world, as you'll see on page 102.

Taylor's father Scott was a financial advisor with his own company. Her mother Andrea was an advertising marketing executive until Taylor was born, after which she became a homemaker. Her middle name Alison was given in honour of her mother's older sister.

When Scott bought a Christmas tree plantation from one of his clients, the family moved a few miles to the town of Wyomissing where Taylor and her young brother Austin had an idyllic early upbringing. "I had the most magical childhood, running free and going anywhere I wanted to in my head," she has said.

⌃ **Taylor (back row, third from right) at the Alvernia Montessori School kindergarten in March 1995 when she was five years old.** *MediaNews Group/ Reading Eagle via Getty Images*

Taylor's grandmother, Marjorie Finlay, neé Moehlenkamp, in 1951, winning a talent contest in connection with the radio show *Music with the Girls. Public domain*

a contract with a radio station to learn her craft. Taylor won an audition to sing *America the Beautiful* at the US Open Tennis Championship in 2002 where she drew the attention of music manager Dan Dymtrow. He helped Taylor win an artist development contract at an RCA Records showcase event in 2003 which was her start in professional music.

In between, 12-year-old Taylor learnt the guitar and played and sang at a coffee shop in Stone Harbour called Coffee Talk during the school holidays. "I always wanted to know, and I always used to daydream, about what it would be like to stand on a really big stage and sing songs for a lot of people, songs that I had written..."

⌄ **Number 76 Grandview Boulevard in Wyomissing, Taylor's childhood home before the move to Hendersonville.** *Shuvaev/CC BY-SA 4.0*

Monster In Her Closet

When she was in 4th grade, Taylor won a national poetry competition through her school, which demonstrated an already mature grasp of rhyme and rhythm. It was also clearly the beginning of a tradition of writing about what matters most to her – love, loss, relationships... and fearlessness.

Monster in my Closet
by Taylor Swift (aged nine)

There's a monster in my closet and I don't know what to do!
Have you ever seen him?
Has he ever pounced on you?
I wonder what he looks like!
Is he purple with red eyes?
I wonder what he likes to eat.
What about his size!!
Tonight I'm gonna catch him!
I'll set a real big trap!
Then I'll train him really well.
He'll answer when I clap!

When I looked up in that closet, there was nothing there but stuff.
I know that monster's in there!
I heard him huff and puff!
Could it be he wants to eat me?
Maybe I'm his favorite tray.
And if he comes to get me,
I'll scream loudly, "Go away!!"
If he's nice, I'll name him "Happy."
If he's bad I'll name him "Grouch."
I suspect that he is leaving, but if not. . .I'll kick him out!

Swiftipedia Taylor Swift Wiki Creative Commons CC-BY-SA

Music In Her Blood

It was a perfect nurturing ground for the imagination that would lead to her successful songwriting career. The family had a second home in Stone Harbor, New Jersey where they often spent the summers. However, despite being clever and pretty, Taylor did not have a wide circle of friends at school and often felt left out. Her focus on her songwriting and singing set her apart from most of her classmates' interests.

There was music in her background. Her grandmother, Marjorie Finlay, was a popular opera star in the 1960s and when Taylor was little she lived with the family in Wyomissing. She was an inspiration to the budding songster and their lives mirrored each other. Marjorie won a talent content in 1950 and the prize was

The move to the capital of country music was the beginning of a rapid rise in young Taylor's musical career and her first taste of fame.

« At the 2006 Academy of Country Music Awards in Las Vegas, Nevada.
Jeff Kravitz/FilmMagic, Inc

A Star in Nash

In 2003, when Taylor was 13, life changed for her in many ways. Her grandmother died and the family moved again, this time to Hendersonville in Tennessee, close to Nashville. It enabled Taylor to pursue her dream to be part of the country music scene. "I think I first realised I wanted to be in country music and be an artist when I was 10," says Taylor. "And I started dragging my parents to festivals and fairs and karaoke contests, and I did that for about a year before I came to Nashville for the first time. I was 11 and I had this demo CD of me singing Dixie Chicks and LeAnne Rimes songs."

The move meant leaving Pennsylvania halfway through her junior high school years but being at the heart of a music-making industry gave Taylor's song writing a massive boost. Her artist development contract with RCA Records was restricting in that it was expected that she would record the work of other artists until she was 18 when she could release some of her own work. "It's like, a guy saying that he wants to date you but not be your boyfriend," she explained later. "You know, they don't wanna sign you to an actual record deal or put an album out on you. They wanna watch your progress for a year.

"It was my job after school every day for two years. I had this little office in the hall, and I was writing songs based on what other people might cut.

It really immersed me in the gorgeous songwriting community, and I've never forgotten what it's like to write for a job."

On Her Way

The RCA deal did get her lots of opportunities to sing in public and an introduction to, and lasting relationship with, country music composer Liz Rose. The two met regularly on a Tuesday afternoon after school to perfect her writing. According to Rose: "She thinks different. I can't tell you what it's like to be in a room with her. There are a lot of great songwriters in the world, but she is one of a few. I know that she's the biggest star in the world, but she's a songwriter first."

ville

Taylor was performing in an industry showcase at The Bluebird Café in Nashville when she was seen by record executive Scott Borchetta, who was looking to launch the label that became Big Machine Records. Tay walked away from her development deal and became his first signing. Her debut album, *Taylor Swift*, was released in October 2006 and earned her a nomination for Best New Artist at the following year's Grammy Awards.

Her next album, *Fearless*, released in 2009, cemented her Grammy fame as it earned eight nominations and four awards in 2010 – Album of the Year, Best Female Country Vocal Performance, Best Country Song and Best Country Album.

⌃ **Performing songs from her *Taylor Swift* debut album, live at the Sound Advice Amphitheater in West Palm Beach in 2007.** *Minds-eye CC AS 2.0*

⌃« **Arriving on the red carpet for the 2007 American Music Awards where she had been nominated as Favorite Country Female Artist.** *Paul Smith/Featureflash*

» **With Scott Borchetta of Big Machine Records, her long-time record producer until they fell out over the sale of her music masters.** *Rick Diamond/ACMA2014/ Getty Images*

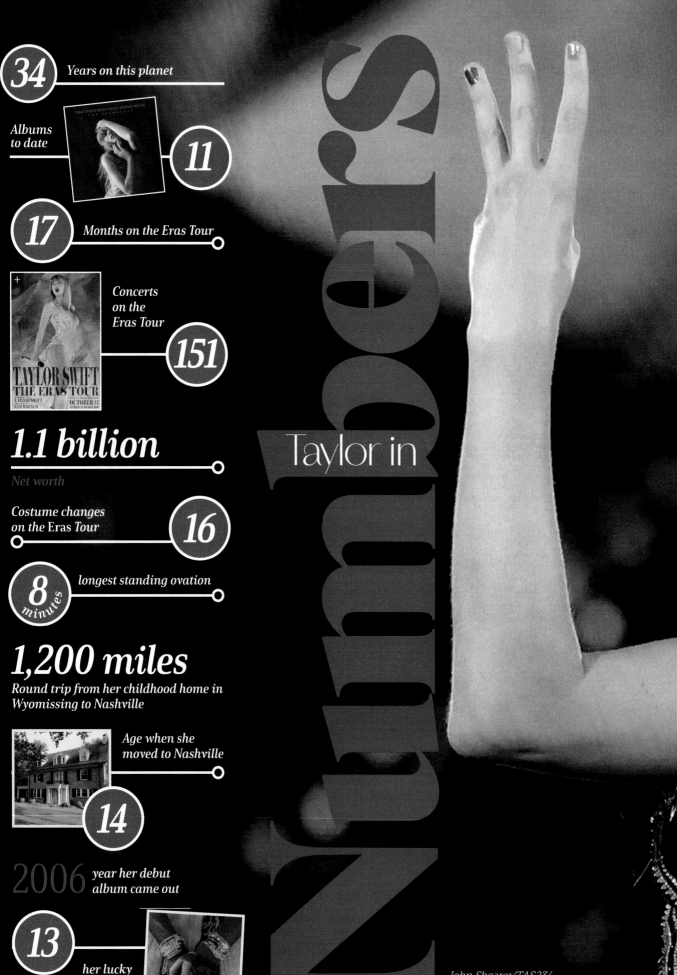

Taylor in Numbers

34 *Years on this planet*

Albums to date **11**

17 *Months on the Eras Tour*

Concerts on the Eras Tour **151**

1.1 billion
Net worth

Costume changes on the Eras Tour **16**

8 *minutes* *longest standing ovation*

1,200 miles
Round trip from her childhood home in Wyomissing to Nashville

Age when she moved to Nashville **14**

2006 *year her debut album came out*

13 *her lucky number, of course!*

John Shearer/TAS23/ Getty Images

113,190,000

Monthly listeners on Spotify

How long it took to write Love Story

20 minutes

Cats who share Taylor's life

3

Serious boyfriends

12

6 years
Longest relationship to date

Grammy Awards

14

774
Total worldwide award wins to date

118
Guinness World Records

313,700,000

Spotify downloads of The Tortured Poets Department on the first day

2022

Year she became a Doctor of Fine Arts

$100,000

Bonuses given to truck drivers working the US leg of the Eras Tour

52
Taylor Swift trademarked phrases, including Shake it Off, Swiftmas, and Taymoji

After releasing the Fearless album, Taylor was well on her way to becoming one of the most famous names in popular music.

Becoming a Supers

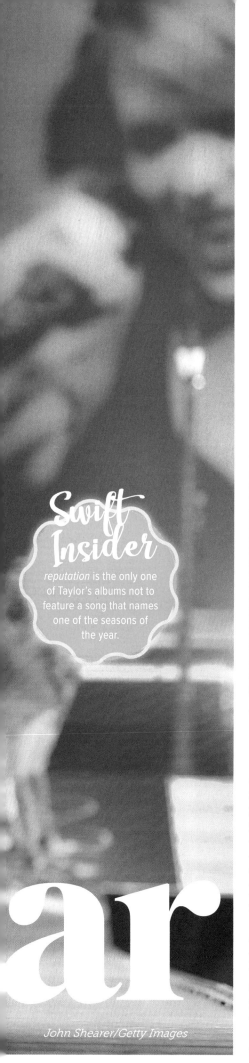

Kanye, Kim & Kancellation

In 2009, at the age of 19 and with her career really taking off, Taylor won an award for Best Female Video at the MTV Video Music Awards. Just as she began her acceptance speech, nervous and in awe of achieving such a high-profile tribute to her work, rapper Kanye West jumped on stage and took the microphone from her. He said: *"Yo, Taylor, I'mma really happy for you and I'mma let you finish, but Beyoncé had one of the best videos of all time!"*

Despite the shock and embarrassment, Taylor conducted herself with dignity. It was a heavily criticised move by West and he eventually said sorry, but then complained Taylor didn't defend him or tell people he'd apologised.

The resentment lingered on both sides and in 2016 West wrote a song called *Famous*, with a nasty lyric about feeling he and Taylor might still have sex. He asserted that he was the one who'd made her famous and the accompanying video contained faked images of Tay lying naked in bed with a crowd of people.

West said she's approved him name-dropping her in a phone call, she said she didn't. West's partner Kim Kardashian called her a snake and Tay ended up being #canceled by the couple's supporters on social media. It caused Taylor to disappear from the public eye for the best part of a year but in 2017 she came roaring back with *reputation*, a biting album full of revenge songs.

Kevin Mazur/
WireImage

Swift Insider

reputation is the only one of Taylor's albums not to feature a song that names one of the seasons of the year.

By 2010 Taylor was writing all the tracks on her albums by herself. She had penned more than 75 songs by the time she released *Speak Now* and was moving further away from the country music style to explore different genres. In many other singers a change of musical types could be dangerous in losing them the support of their original fan base, but Taylor's Swifties have always been right behind her wherever she has taken her music.

So from a pure country sound on her debut album she moved to country-pop with her crossover album *Fearless*, then pop-rock mixed with a smidgin of country on *Speak Now*, which also introduced a more theatrical style of videos to support it.

She experimented with folk combined with pop-rock on *Red* but *1989* was straight pop, inspired by the music of the 1980s and her stage show reflected the fashions of the day with crop tops and flared mini skirts. *reputation* had an altogether raunchier electropop and R&B sound, suiting the darker, more aggressive lyrics. *Lover* returned to the gentler celebration of romance with ballads and fun, poppy songs.

The pandemic albums *folklore* and *evermore* took Taylor into more of an indie vibe mixed with folk. These were simpler and thoughtful, with *folklore* evoking the summer season and *evermore* the winter. Post-pandemic, Taylor gave us *Midnights* and its softer pop themes and finally *The Tortured Poets Department*, which returned to darker themes of dealing with fame and heartbreak and the pressures of living in the public eye, but still with some optimistic tracks looking to the future.

Asserting Her Rights

In 2019, Taylor's world was jolted by the sale of her record label and the masters to her studio albums to a business entrepreneur.

When Taylor agreed a recording deal with Big Machine Records in 2005 her contract tied her in for 13 years. She would produce a series of albums and in return she would get a cash advance in anticipation of the money they would make. She kept the publishing rights – lyrics and melodies – which meant she would be free to re-record the songs after a fixed period. But the rights to the masters – the sound recordings of the final products – belonged to the record company, which was standard practice for recording artists at the time.

In 2018 the end of her contract was approaching and her management team, which included her parents, asked for the masters to be sold back to her. Big Machine Record's proposed renewal contract said that the masters to one old album would be returned to her each time she recorded a new one. She refused to agree to that arrangement and so when her old contract expired she signed with Republic Records instead.

Before any further negotiations on ownership of her masters could happen, her trusted mentor Scott Borchetta sold the Big Machine company to Ithaca Holdings. That company belonged to music entrepreneur Scooter Braun, who Taylor had an issue with because of his alleged encouragement of the Kanye West/Kim Kardashian feud. Borchetta stayed on as CEO of the new company but he was no longer the person to whom Taylor would report.

With the sale went the masters of Taylor's first six albums from *Taylor Swift* to *reputation*. She therefore lost all control of them, and to perform any of those songs she had to get permission from Braun. This apparently wasn't granted for the 2019 American Music Awards, where she won Artist of the Decade, or her documentary *Miss Americana* in 2020. So she didn't perform any of her by now familiar tracks for either of them.

Braun went on to sell the masters to a private equity company, Shamrock Holdings, the major shareholder of which was Roy Disney, brother of the famous Walt. Having failed to have the opportunity to buy them, Taylor turned down all offers of collaboration with the new owners.

Losing control over her own musical performances was an unacceptable situation and Taylor engineered the perfect solution. In 2020, then free from the original Big Machine Company's contract, she revisited her earlier albums one by one, updating them, adding tracks and releasing them as *Taylor's Versions*.

The extra songs, taken out of an imaginary strong-room, were called Vault tracks. These were songs that would not fit on the

Scott Borchetta (left) and Scooter Braun announcing the sale of Big Machine Records to Braun's company Ithaca Holdings.
Kevin Mazur/Getty Images

Dream Result

In 2021 a slow zoom trend began on TikTok with fans lip-syncing to Taylor's *Wildest Dreams* from the album *1989*. The craze led to 735,000 plays on Spotify in a single day, the largest number of one-day streams in the history of the platform.

Two days later Taylor released *Wildest Dreams (Taylor's Version)* with her own snippet on TikTok inviting people to use her re-recording for their slow zooms, rather than the original.

Fans responded big time and the new version was streamed 2,003,391 times in just four hours — a record-smashing result!

original albums and she had tucked them away for future release. The assertive move to take back control was a first for the music industry. It brought to everyone's attention what had long been common practice for a lot of artists. She paved the way for more singer/songwriters to keep the rights to their studio recordings as well as their lyrics and melodies.

A two-part documentary about the dispute between Tay and Scooter Braun aired in the UK on the Discovery + channel in June 2024.

Julien de Rosa/AFP

Looking Back Over the Eras

After topping world charts repeatedly with 10 albums, it was time for Taylor to sum up her career so far by launching the Eras Tour.

It began in March 2023 and will end in December 2024. The world's biggest musical tour has been racking up global statistics and world records, adding money to countries' economies and making billions in merchandise and music sales. It has a best-selling supporting concert movie shown in cinemas and then on TV around the world.

It has also provided the first chance in five years for Taylor's many, many fans to come together in concert halls and movie theatres, dress up in sparkly clothes, exchange friendship bracelets, and make themselves hoarse singing the lyrics to all the songs, with lots of set-piece actions to go along with them.

After touring through 2023 and the first three months of 2024, Taylor took a month's break and surprise-released *The Tortured Poets Department*. This led to some changes in the rundown for her remaining 2024 concerts to accommodate some of the new tracks, and she made some costume changes too.

The new order of songs started with the first Paris concert on May 9.

❯ *Kevin Mazur/TAS24/Getty Images*

Ignisign/dreamstime.com

WELCOME TO THE ERAS TOUR, AUSTRALIA

LOVER ERA
Miss Americana & The Heartbreak Prince
Cruel Summer
The Man
You Need To Calm Down (short version)
Lover

FEARLESS ERA
Fearless (short version)
You Belong With Me
Love Story

RED ERA
22
We Are Never Ever Getting Back Together
I Knew You Were Trouble
All Too Well (10 Minute Version)

SPEAK NOW ERA
Enchanted

REPUTATION ERA
...Ready For It?
Delicate
Don't Blame Me
Look What You Made Me Do

FOLKLORE AND EVERMORE ERA
cardigan
betty
champagne problems
august
illicit affairs (short version)
my tears ricochet
marjorie (short version)
willow

1989 ERA
Style
Blank Space
Shake It Off
Wildest Dreams (short version)
Bad Blood (short version)

THE TORTURED POETS DEPARTMENT ERA
But Daddy I Love Him
So High School (short version)
Who's Afraid of Little Old Me?
Down Bad
Fortnight
The Smallest Man Who Ever Lived
I Can Do it With a Broken Heart

GUITAR ACOUSTIC
Songs such as: Mine; Say Don't Go; ME!; Afterglow; New Romantics; Stay Stay Stay; Message In A Bottle; Starlight; Picture To Burn

PIANO ACOUSTIC
Songs such as: It's Time To Go; Would've, Could've, Should've; So It Goes; Maroon; New Year's Day; All Of The Girls You Loved Before; Tied Together With A Smile; Back To December; Timeless

MIDNIGHTS ERA
Lavender Haze
Anti-Hero
Midnight Rain
Vigilante Shit
Bejeweled
Mastermind
Karma

Swift Insider
When listening to Red, join in the chorus of We are Never Ever Getting Back Together by singing "Like Ever!" very loudly.

Background image: Kiwnug on Unsplash

Who's Who
in Taylor's Life

Family, friends, boyfriends and colleagues, all the people who have made an impact on Taylor's life have made her the woman she is today.

Christopher Polk/ TAS/Getty Images

Family

⌃ Austin Swift: Taylor's younger brother, who is her staunch supporter. *Kathy Hutchins/shutterstock*
» Scott and Andrea Swift: Taylor's parents, who gave her an idyllic childhood and every opportunity to pursue her dream to be a singer/songwriter. *RB/Bauer-Griffin/GC Images;Rick Diamond/Getty Images*

Friends

⌃ Ed Sheeran: Friend/colleague, a collaborator on a number of Taylor's songs, performer at some of her gigs and a buddy to hang out with at her New York and Rhode Island homes. *Gareth Cattermole/TAS/Getty Image*

» Selina Gomez: Met Taylor when they were both dating Jonas brothers. Pictured on Taylor's left with Brittany Mahomes. Gigi Hadid and Sophie Turner following behind. *Gotham/GC Images*

« Abigail Anderson Berard Taylor's best friend from high school who shared her isolation from the 'in' crowd. *Kevin Mazur/WireImage*

⌄ Blake Lively and Ashley Avignone (pictured on Taylor's left and right) with Ice Spice. Just some of the high profile celebs who make up Taylor's 'Squad'. *Steph Chambers/Getty Images*

Colleagues

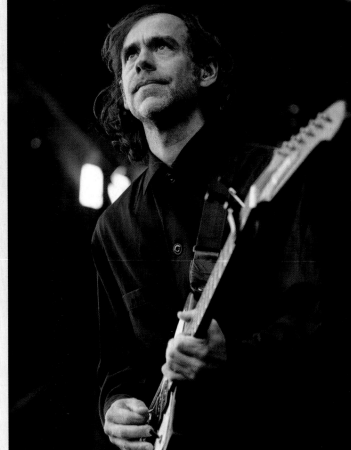

» Tree Paine: Taylor's publicist, who has guided her through the ups and downs of fame and established her loyal fan base. Pictured, left, with Taylor and singer/songwriter Halsey at the 2019 American Music Awards. *Emma McIntyre/AMA2019/Getty Images*

» Liz Rose: Country music specialist who coached Taylor in songwriting back at the beginning of her career and co-wrote many of her early songs, including *You Belong With Me*. *Kevin Winter/Getty Images*

» Aaron Dessner: Musician who worked with Taylor on her pandemic albums, *folklore* and *evermore* and continues to collaborate to this day. *Taylor Creek Media/dreamstime.com*

Boyfriends

⌃« Jake Gyllenhaal: They met later in 2010 at a dinner party hosted by actor Gwyneth Paltrow and her husband, singer/songwriter Chris Martin, but despite their romance being intense for a while, it didn't last. *Munawar Hosain/Fotos International/Getty Images*

⌃ John Mayer: The singer was quite a bit older than Taylor and judging by the lyrics in her song Dear John, she felt that he didn't take her seriously when she was very much in love in early 2010. *Theo Wargo/WireImage*

« Calvin Harris: The Scottish DJ who found being Taylor's boyfriend for a year between March 2015 and June 2016 too hard to handle because of the media circus that followed them around. *Alo Ceballos/GC Images*

⌃ Tom Hiddleston Another older man but this relationship ended on a friendlier footing after four months in summer 2016. *Starstock/dreamstime.com*

« Joe Alwyn: Taylor's longest beau to date. They were together for six years but grew apart, perhaps due to the permanent media spotlight on them. *Jackson Lee/GC Images*

» Travis Kelce: The American footballer who has captured Taylor's heart in September 2023, who backs her to the hilt and, in turn, has her support at almost every game. *Jerry Coli/dreamstime.com*

Taylor teamed up with brother Austin (pictured) and producer Jack Antonoff to form a pretend band and record a track for the TV series **Killing Eve**. *Charley Gallay/Getty Images*

⌃ Celebrating at the end of a Kansas City Chiefs game in January 2024. *Jamie Squire/Getty Images* « Hiking outside Los Angeles with her pal Gigi Hadid and her ever-present bodyguard. *MPI99/Bauer-Griffin/GC Images*

Life Outside Music

When she is not writing, performing or recording music, Taylor lives the life of an average 30-something woman, albeit one who has a spotlight permanently turned on her!

⌃ **Indulging in a hot dog while watching the filming of the Jonas Brothers' video in 2008.** *Everett Collection/shutterstock*

Spending almost two years on tour, performing 151 three-hour shows, requires a high level of physical stamina. Taylor's fitness regime before and during the tour, in the breaks between blocks of concerts, had to go up a notch. Personal trainer Kirk Myers, who runs gyms in New York and Los Angeles, was the man in charge. "We approached her training for the Eras tour with the mindset like a professional athlete," he said. "There was an 'off-season' when she wasn't touring and 'in-season' when she was."

In the off-season, six months before the start of the tour, Taylor was in the gym a couple of hours a day, six days a week, working on strength and conditioning. "Every day I would run on the treadmill," she said, "singing the entire set list out loud – fast for fast songs, and a jog or a fast walk for slow songs."

On-seasons were a little less strenuous. "We would average two times a week," said Myers. "In-season training was more about maintenance… stability, mobility, biomechanics."

With choreographer Mandy Moore, Taylor additionally worked on her dance moves. "I had three months of dance training because I wanted to get it in my bones," she said. "I wanted to be so over-rehearsed that I could be silly with the fans, and not lose my train of thought."

Aside from the gym and studio work, Taylor is a fan of hiking. "I'm very much out in the world, and I love exploring the places we go when we tour. It's important for me to live a full life." And she enjoys a game of pickleball, a sport with paddles and a plastic ball combining lawn tennis, table tennis and badminton.

Food

Taylor has a time-and-place approach to eating. "During the week, I try to eat healthily, so that means salads, yogurt, and sandwiches," she has said. "No sugary drinks. I try to keep it lighter, but it's nothing too regimented or crazy. I don't like to create too many rules where I don't need them." At the weekends, "I allow myself to eat what I know from common sense is bad for me. I love a burger and fries, I love ice cream so much, and I love baking cookies. Actually, I love baking anything." 'Anything' includes apple pie, sheet cake or tray bakes, and cupcakes, along with pumpkin bread and birthday cakes for friends.

"Cooking has been my escape from stress and one of the only ways I can truly calm myself on a rough day," she said. "I love making an entire meal, starting from making iced tea in a pitcher and then making tomato mozzarella pesto paninis." She boasts of whipping up "a mean barbecue chicken and really great pasta dishes, shrimp scampi and a great chicken with capers."

Eating out, particularly in New York, is enjoyed with friends and partners. In 2023 Eater, an online food and dining brand, compiled a list of restaurants Taylor had been spotted at. Her preference seems to be for Asian – Koi New York (Japanese), Nobu Fifty Seven (sushi), and Lure Fishbar (dim sum). And she also loves Italians – Locanda Verde (co-owned by actor Robert De Niro), Lucali (pizzeria), Emilio's Ballato and Il Buco Alimentari & Vineria.

Swift Insider

Jack Leopards & The Dolphin Club was a fake indie band that Taylor, her brother Austin, and producer Jack Antonoff formed to sing *Look What You Made Me Do* for the TV show Killing Eve

Holiday time at Hyannisport, Massachusetts in 2012.
Robert Scott Button/shutterstock

Homes

Having a bolthole is important for a mega star and Taylor also needs a place to entertain family and friends and make a home for her cats. She bought her first apartment in Nashville, but now mostly lives in a New York townhouse and next-door penthouse in Lower Manhattan.

To escape the heat and noise of the city, Taylor bought a spacious colonial-style mansion called Holiday House at Watch Hill in Rhode Island state, three hours' drive from central New York. It is positioned at the highest point on the peninsula above a long stretch of shoreline and overlooking the tip of Long Island.

This is where she has held several high-profile Taymerica Fourth of July parties for celebrity friends as well as her touring staff. The latest was in 2023 with outdoor games, inflatable slide, sparklers, and red, white and blue onesies for guests to wear.

This is the mansion Taylor sings about in the *last great american dynasty* – an ode to eccentric Standard Oil heiress Rebekah Harkness who used to own the house – and the video of the song features the view of the sea and beach from the garden.

In 2012, it was rumoured that Taylor had bought another seafront property in Hyannisport, Massachusetts, next door to the compound owned by the famous Kennedy family. At the time she was going out with Conor Kennedy, grandson of the late Senator Robert Kennedy. Unfortunately, the end of the romance seems to have meant the end of the house as it was sold again later the same year.

Cats

Taylor's love of her cats is well known. Doctor Meredith Grey, Detective Olivia Benson and Benjamin Button have special places in her heart. The three famous fur babies are well travelled, accompanying Taylor in their personalised cat carriers between her homes and even on tour if she's going places without strict quarantine rules. "Meredith is one of the best cats," Taylor said of the oldest member of the household. "She doesn't leave fur or furballs and she is never aggressive or

Swift Insider

Tay hosted listening get-togethers with groups of fans, called Secret Sessions, at her Rhode Island seaside home, to get their feedback before the release of the *1989* and *reputation* albums

The converted Sugar Loaf warehouse in Franklin Street, New York where Taylor has an apartment, and the townhouse next door to the left that she also owns. *Russ Ross Photography/therussross.com*

afraid of being around people."

Olivia, a white Scottish Fold, arrived in 2014. "Her name in the house is Dibbles," said Taylor, "because it suits her personality more than Olivia. She's like a scrappy little cat."

Last, but not least, on the scene came the Ragdoll cat with bandit markings, Benjamin Button. He was brought to the 2019 shoot for Taylor's video ME! to play the part of a peace-offering from the male character in the story, played by Brendon Urie. But in real life he went home with Taylor and living happily ever after with his step-sisters.

Charity

Taylor is known for making donations out of the blue to charities and individuals struggling financially or medically. Fans have been helped to cover college fees, rent arrears and medical bills. During Covid she helped out people whose jobs disappeared when their employers had to downsize and families that had lost the main breadwinner to the disease.

Making a positive impact on education she endowed the Taylor Swift Education Center at the Nashville Country Music Hall of Fame and Museum with a $4 million donation. The center gives disadvantaged children the chance to learn to play musical instruments. And she donated $70,000 in books to her hometown library and 6,000 books to the Reading Public Library in Pennsylvania. The proceeds from the sale of *Welcome to New York* from the *1989* album went to New York city schools.

Lately, Taylor has been helping Brittany Mahomes, wife of the Kansas City Chief's quarterback Patrick, with the Mahomies Foundation charity dedicated to improving the lives of children. She has also given her time to fundraisers for Children in Need, Stand Up 2 Cancer and mental health charities.

Most recently she has helped people affected by a huge tornado in her home state of Tennessee in December 2023. This was on top of money given to help after catastrophic storms in Louisiana in 2016, Houston, Texas, in 2017 and Nashville in 2020.

In February 2024, when the Kansas City Chiefs were on a victory parade in their home town, a gunman killed radio DJ Lisa Lopez-Galvan and wounded 22 others. Taylor sent $100,000 to a GoFundMe on behalf of Lisa's family. And the same month, on the Australian leg of the Eras tour, she did what has become a hallmark of the tour and gave money to a local foodbank.

Benjamin Button is a cute ragdoll cat and one of Taylor's three furry babies. *Nils Jacobi/shutterstock*

Taylor's white Holiday House, standing above the shoreline on Rhode Island. *Carol Ann Mossa/ shutterstock*

Dating

Tay has always protected the most personal parts of her life carefully. However, if you're Taylor Swift your boyfriends are most likely celebrities themselves and keeping things quiet is almost impossible.

In 2008, her first high-profile date was Joe Jonas of the Jonas Brothers band. She and her BFF actor and singer Selena Gomez both dated a Jonas brother. Tay and Joe were together for three months after which he dumped her in a 27-second phone call she was quite up-front about. She wrote the track *Forever & Always* on the *Fearless* album about it.

Joe was followed by actor Taylor Lautner, who she met on the film *Valentine's Day*. Fans quickly nicknamed them Taylor Squared. It's rumoured he was fonder of her than she was of him so they only lasted four months. She wrote *Back to December* and *Apologize* by way of apology.

Then came musician John Mayer, a decade older than Tay. There are at least six songs alleged to be about him. *Dear John* has bitter lyrics about a man who treats his women cruelly that Mayer was reported to have been angry about.

Actor Jake Gyllenhaal went in for elaborate gestures when they were dating, apparently once flying her in a private jet to meet him. But he didn't turn up for her 21st birthday party and later broke up with her in a text message. *All Too Well*, that Taylor made into a short film, was about him.

She wrote quite a few songs that could be said to allude to her unhappy endings with singer Harry Styles and DJ songwriter and producer Calvin Harris. She and Styles had what purported to be a terminal disagreement when they were on vacation in the Caribbean and she left for home early. They later made up and are friends again now.

Calvin Harris kept Taylor's heart for over a year and they wrote *This is What You Came For* together for Rhianna. Their break-up was very public, seemingly based on creative jealousy and Calvin's aversion to being part of a media circus.

Before her relationship with Calvin was properly over, Taylor met British actor Tom Hiddleston at the Met Gala Ball in New York, fresh from his success in TV's *The Night Manager*. They dated over the summer of 2016

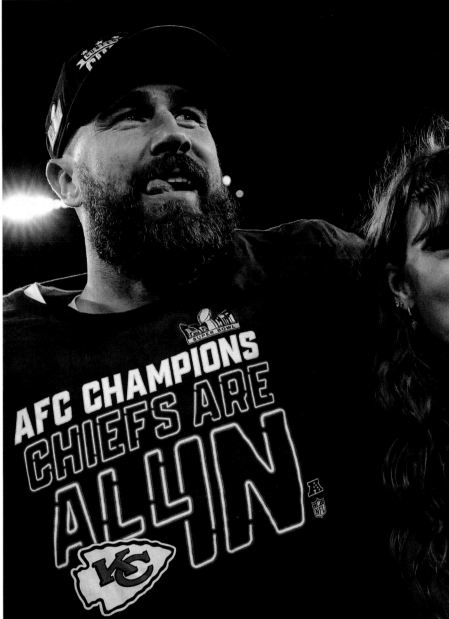

Sailing in Hannis Harbor with Conor Kennedy and friends the summer the couple were dating in 2012. *Robert Scott Button/shutterstock*

Not exactly out of the limelight, but enjoying time out from touring with boyfriend Travis Kelce at the end of one of his games. *Patrick Smith/Getty Images*

and Tay wrote *Getaway Car* and *Midnight Rain* that could be about him.

Her longest relationship to date was with British actor Joe Alwyn. They were together for six years and fans were all set for a marriage announcement, but it was not to be. They kept their relationship out of the limelight and refused to talk about each other in interviews. More than 14 of her songs have been analysed to be about Joe.

That breakup was supposedly followed by a very brief love affair with Matt Healy of The 1975 band. At least one of the tracks on *The Tortured Poets Department* is potentially about their short time together.

Taylor's latest love is Travis Kelce, Kansas City Chiefs Tight End. Between the Paris concerts on the Eras tour and the Stockholm ones the couple spent some 'us' time at Italy's Lake Como. He has been at many of the Eras concerts and Taylor has been very vocally supporting him at games during the football season.

The 'T & T effect' has brought many more fans to the game of American football and has lifted Swifties' spirits again, wondering if maybe this time he is *The 1.*

Friends

There's a group of people who have become known as Taylor's Squad. They live in the celebrity world so they give Taylor reality checks in private but endless support in public. Members of the Squad are musicians, actors, designers, models, media experts. Some she has known for years, some have joined quite recently, but all of them are

die-hard Swifties. There are actors Blake Lively and Lena Dunham, models Gigi Hadid, Cara Delevingne and Martha Hunt, jewellery designer Claire Kislinger, singer Ed Sheeran, YouTube king Todrick Hall and Tay's publicist Tree Paine, has helped her to build her loyal fan base.

One of Taylor's oldest connections is with Abigail Anderson Berard, who has been a friend since high school. They are often seen together, most recently on the Nashville leg of the Eras tour where Tay sang *Fifteen* in the surprise acoustic section, the song she wrote for Abigail.

Long-standing music BFF Selina Gomez met Taylor in 2005 and they have been close ever since. Almost as lengthy has been her friendship with stylist Ashley Avignone. She was introduced to Tay by actor Emma Stone, who got buddy with her at an awards event in 2008. Emma also played matchmaker when she introduced Taylor to Joe Alwyn.

Taylor's New York apartment is a popular hangout for her closest friends – a place where she can bake cookies for them or order in pizza to sit around and listen to music in their pyjamas. It's there that she has held New Year's Eve fancy dress parties and invited friends to share her birthday celebrations. Her Rhode Island holiday home has seen many fun Fourth of July parties to which not only the Squad but also many of the tour dancers and business staff have been invited.

The Squad is important to Taylor as a defence force when the world gets tough. They're mates to share the ups and downs of life with and an inspiration for her music.

⌃ **Taylor Squared – Taylor and Taylor Lautner on a date in 2009.** *Jean Baptiste Lacroix/WireImage* « **One of Taylor's Squad, Todrick Hall, with her backstage at the musical Kinky Boots in New York in 2016.** *Bruce Glikas/Getty Images*

Dressed to Impress

Awards evenings, premieres, all manner of red carpet events and you can guarantee Taylor will appear looking like a million dollars.

The world's top designers line up to dress Taylor in their up-to-date fashions and provide accessories to delight all fashionistas. Some of the star's outfits have a timeless quality, others are very much of their era. Some have been outstanding successes – and, let's face it, hardly anyone could wear clothes as well as she does – others perhaps best forgotten or written off as products of that time. But as Taylor says: "Fashion is all about playful experimentation. If you don't look back at pictures of some of your old looks and cringe, you're doing it wrong."

» **Joining Emma Stone at the 2010 Los Angeles premiere of Emma's *Easy A* film. Taylor in a Miu Miu silk bustier dress with Neil Lane jewellery and Christian Louboutin shoes; Emma in an Emilio Pucci mini dress and Stella McCartney heels.**
Starstock /dreamstime.com

« **For the Country Music Awards in 2009 Taylor was Fearless in a stand-out Angel Sanchez dress and Neil Lane jewellery.**
Carrienelson/dreamstime.com

Swift Insider

If you study Taylor's outfits at public events through the years you see a subtle echo of the era of her latest album – clever couture!

For the 2020 Golden Globe Awards Taylor chose a flowing floral Etro dress and Lorraine Schwartz jewellery, foretelling her folklore era perhaps?
Featureflash/ dreamstime.com

» At the premiere of *The Giver* movie in 2014 in a Monique Lhuillier gown and Casadei heels. *Dwong19/dreamstime.com*

» A Versace body suit, shorts and blazer were the colourful choice for the 2019 Teen Choice Awards in Los Angeles, teamed with sandals by Kat Maconie. Taylor wore a lot of Maconie shoes while she was promoting her *Lover* album. *Hutchinsphoto/dreamstime.com*

» The white strapless Schiaparelli gown, black opera gloves, Giuseppe Zanotti heels and Lorraine Schwartz clockface choker heralded the announcement of the release of *The Tortured Poets Department* album at the 2024 Grammy Awards ceremony. *Jeff Kravitz/FilmMagic*

⌃ Wearing a J Mendel suit for the 2012 MTV Video Music Awards in Los Angeles. *Featureflash/dreamstime.com*

» Going for a rockier 1989 look at the 2015 MTV Video Awards in an Ashish crop top and joggers and Christian Louboutin shoes. *Press Line Photos/shutterstock*

» The Grammy Awards in 2015 called for an Elie Saab gown and contrasting pink Giuseppe Zanotti heels. *DFree/shutterstock*
⌄ Taylor posed for a fashion shoot in Canadian Elle magazine in 2012 and this glorious Marchesa tulle dress matched with Giuseppe Zanotti shoes stole the show. *Pixabay Creative Commons*

« In a Zuhair Murad gown to perform *Mean* at the 2012 Grammy Awards – a song about growing up and pitying the school bully called for a sophisticated look. *Featureflash/dreamstime.com*

⌃ In the light-hearted *Lover* era, a Rosa Bloom sequinned romper suit and Sophia Webster butterfly heels were the choice for the 2019 iHeartRadio Music Awards. *Featureflash/shutterstock*

⌐ The choice for the 2014 MTV Video Music Awards was Greek fashion designer Mary Katrantzou's body suit and Elie Saab booties. *Starstock/dreamstime.com*

« At the 2013 Golden Globe Awards in a Donna Karan dress accessorised with Lorraine Schwartz earrings. *Featureflash/dreamstime.com*

The Albums

Taylor's musical career has seen her shine in many different genres. The resulting 15 albums, each one building on previous successes, have taken the listener on a diverse journey.

2006
TAYLOR SWIFT

On Taylor's first album seven of the 11 tracks were written in collaboration with country songwriter Liz Rose, the others were Tay's alone. *The Outside* was the first song she ever wrote, at the age of 12, and it talks about being an outcast at school. The whole album is the perfect picture of a teenage girl dealing with relationships and trying to find the confidence to grow and assert herself.

The music was in the country style and featured heartbreak songs such as *Tim McGraw*, about a boy she was dating who left her when he went away to college. She wrote it during her maths class in the first year of junior high and the whole album was recorded in the afternoons, after school was finished for the day.

Teardrops on My Guitar and *Our Song* were written about a boy she liked but never actually got to date because he didn't know she had a crush on him. With the single *Our Song* she became the youngest singer/songwriter to reach Number 1 in the *Billboard* magazine country charts. The Academy of Country Music named her Top New Female Vocalist in 2007 and the real-life country singer Tim McGraw and his wife Faith Hill invited Taylor to be an opening act on their tour that year.

» Al Messerschmidt/ Getty Images
« Featureflash/ dreamstime.com
Background image: Luke Besley/Unsplash

Swift Insider

The video of *Tim McGraw* has been viewed more than 25 million times on YouTube.

The Fearless album was a move away from country music and into the world of pop. *You Belong With Me* is a song from a different perspective – Taylor's sympathy for a boy who wants a girl who's ignoring him. The accompanying video won at the 2009 MTV Video Music Awards and Kanye West famously stole Tay's acceptance speech slot to big-up Beyonce's video for *Single Ladies*. This led to a long-running feud with West and his former wife Kim Kardashian.

Fifteen is about Taylor's high school friend Abigail Anderson. The two friends were outsiders in the school cliques and supported each other. Taylor says the song, "talks about how my best friend, Abigail, got her heart broken when we were in ninth grade, and singing about that absolutely gets me every time."

« *Everett Collection/shutterstock*
» *A Paes/shutterstock*
Background image: Kiwihug/Unsplash

2008 FEARLESS

2021 FEARLESS
(Taylor's Version)

Love Story, written, she says, in about 20 minutes while lying on her bedroom floor, is about Taylor's own relationship but with someone her parents didn't approve of. According to Taylor it was, "A love that you've got to hide because for whatever reason it wouldn't go over well." Some have speculated that the man in question was Joe Jonas of the Jonas brothers.

Taylor was ecstatic when *White Horse* was chosen as background music in the 2008 season opener of *Grey's Anatomy*, one of her favourite TV shows. "You should've seen the tears streaming down my face when I got the phone call that they were going to use that song, I have never been that excited."

Taylor's Version had six extra tracks: *Don't You, You All Over Me, Mr Perfectly Fine, We Were Happy, That's When* and *Bye Bye Baby.*

Taylor's Christmas Special

In 2009 Taylor released an EP of cover songs and two originals, all geared to catch the mood of the holiday season. Called *The Taylor Swift Holiday Collection* it features the classics *White Christmas, Silent Night, Santa Baby* and George Michael's *Last Christmas* as well as two tracks, *Christmases When You Were Mine* and *Christmas Must Be Something More* that Taylor wrote specially.

Swifties have suggested she should now release a Taylor's Version of the mini album with some additions such as *Christmas Tree Farm* and *New Year's Day.*

« Amazon.com

2010
SPEAK NOW

2023
SPEAK NOW
(Taylor's Version)

This was the first of Taylor's albums where she wrote every song by herself, and she did so while touring to promote her *Fearless* album. Moving her music a little closer to a pop-rock style, *Speak Now* focuses on all the words that were left unsaid in previous romantic relationships or difficult encounters – the kind of things you wished you'd voiced at the time but didn't have the nerve.

Two tracks on the album – *Dear John* and *The Story Of Us* – are alleged to be about rock musician John Mayer, a man 13 years

older than Taylor who she dated briefly from late 2009 to early 2010. She related how the man in the songs cruelly played with her emotions. Mayer later commented that he felt humiliated by Taylor, assuming that the song was about him.

The song *Enchanted* is about Adam Young of Owl City and she wrote it after the couple had met for the first time and all she could think of was that she hoped he wasn't in love with someone. The two never dated, although he did later state his interest in her. *Last Kiss* is about her break-up with Joe Jonas, that

she revealed happened in a 27-second phone call. So, of course, the intro to the song is 27 seconds long.

Innocent was inspired directly by what happened to Taylor when Kanye West interrupted the Video Music Awards in 2009. But instead of being about what West had done to her it was written to him with lines such as, "Who you are is not what you did".

Taylor's Version had another six tracks: *Electric Touch, When Emma Falls In Love, I Can See You, Castles Crumbling, Foolish One* and *Timeless.*

Swift Insider

Sparks Fly starts with a reference to a rainstorm; it's one of five songs on *Speak Now* to feature rain. In total Tay has sung about rain on 35 album tracks.

Rick Diamond/Getty Images

Chris McGrath/TAS/Getty Images

2012 RED

2021 RED (Taylor's Version)

With the release of this album and its rockier sound, critics began to write about Taylor as a musical heavy hitter. Having written *Speak Now* entirely by herself, she now approached different producer/singer/songwriters to experiment with new musical styles such as Britrock, dubstep and electronic, that would inject her songs with different sound emotions. Altogether, she worked with 10 different producers to give *Red* its distinctive feel. The album is all about dealing with dangerous and failed romantic relationships.

All Too Well was the first song Taylor wrote for the new album. It was expanded from five to 10 minutes for Taylor's Version and is seen as possibly Taylor's best song. In 2021 *Rolling Stone* magazine named it number 69 in its 500 Greatest Songs of All Time and it won a Song of the Year Grammy Award in 2023.

We Are Never Ever Getting Back Together is a playful pop-y song with a crazy video featuring her band members and dancers dressed in fluffy animal costumes. It

was supposedly written about actor Jake Gyllenhaal and their patchy relationship. The moment that their on-off romance came to an end, when Jake missed her 21st birthday party, was recorded as *The Moment I Knew*.

Treacherous was the big album hit for the critics, particularly as heard on Taylor's Version where they thought her vocals had matured since the first release of *Red*. Drawing influence from a rock style, *The Last Time* saw Taylor join forces with Gary Lightbody and Jacknife Lee of Snow Patrol. And she wrote and sang *Everything Has Changed* with Ed Sheeran, who became a good friend. *Ronan* was written for a little boy who died of neuroblastoma cancer. The lyrics were taken from his mother's blog about his illness and death.

Taylor's Version has the extra tracks: *Better Man, Nothing New, Babe, Message In a Bottle, I Bet You Think About Me, Forever Winter, Run, The Very First Night* and *All Too Well (10 Minute Version)*.

2014
1989

2023
1989
(Taylor's Version)

Steve Granitz/WireImage

Named after Taylor's birth year and containing a few more aggressive, although playful, songs than previous albums, *1989* majored on 80s-style synthesisers and drum machines. It was Tay's first collaboration with producer/musician Jack Antonoff, who worked with her on some of the tracks and has stuck with her ever since. He sent her an instrumental composition for what would become *Out of the Woods* and Taylor wrote the lyrics to it in half an hour. The ominous beat of the music and the shadowy wolves following Taylor in the video give a sense of a rocky relationship with failure just waiting to happen, which it eventually does.

Bad Blood dipped a toe into a new musical genre for Taylor, with lines from rapper Kendrick Lamar. The video looks like a superhero fantasy movie starring many of the people in Taylor's Squad of close friends, such as actor Selena Gomez, singer Ellie Goulding, and models Gigi Hadid and Cara Delevingne. Taylor played a character called Catastrophe.

Blank Space was a direct dig at members of the media who made her sound like a serial dater who never committed to anyone, and *Shake it Off* is her response to what they write. In *Wildest Dreams*, Taylor's heartbeat is heard in amongst the percussion sounds in a song about a dangerous romance. The video starred Scott Eastwood, youngest son of veteran actor Clint Eastwood, as the untrustworthy tough guy. The line "wildest dreams" also appears as a lyric in *This Love*, the first song Tay wrote for *1989*.

The *1989* album was considered by Taylor to be her first official pop album and seven of the tracks were released as singles. These would have been expected to be favourites to stream but the whole album was withheld from these services at a time when there was a concern that artists were not getting any benefit from free streaming. "Music is art, and art is important and rare," Taylor said at the time. "Important, rare things are valuable. Valuable things should be paid for."

Taylor's Version has the extra tracks: *Slut!, Say Don't Go, Now That We Don't Talk, Suburban Legends* and *It Is Over Now?*

Swift Insider

Taylor's cat, Olivia Benson, makes a cameo appearance in the *Blank Space* video. In 2023 she won Favourite Pet in the Kid's Choice Awards on the Nickelodeon TV channel.

Fabio Diena/dreamstime.com

2017
REPUTATION

The *reputation* album dropped as Taylor came out of a low period in her life when she had been 'canceled' on social media because of the ongoing feud with Kanye West and his partner Kim Kardashian. Huge media interest had stemmed from that and Tay's contemporaries in the music and film world had divided into those who supported her and those who sided with West. Her fans remained loyal but the situation threatened to have a bad effect on her mental health, so she largely retreated from public view and began work on *reputation*.

The album has a heavier electropop sound than previous ones, with hip hop and R&B thrown in. It starts on a darker note but by the later tracks it has begun to sound more optimistic, looking to new love and good friendships. *Look What You Made Me Do* is her revenge-taking track where she sings: "But I got

smarter, I got harder in the nick of time / Honey, I rose up from the dead, I do it all the time."

Other dark tracks include *...Ready For It* about doing wrong in an alien world and *End Game*, featuring Ed Sheeran, about having high profile enemies, making mistakes and loving bad boys. By the time we get to *Delicate* and *So It Goes...* the mood is changing with Taylor hoping a new love interest will help her to get back on track and asserting that she is "not a bad girl".

The later songs on the album portray excitement, maturity and assertiveness, shaking off the feelings of being a canceled person. Several of them are thought to be specifically about the boyfriends Tay had at that time, which she celebrates because they are attracted to her despite her bad reputation. *Dancing With Our Hands Tied* is alleged to be about DJ Calvin Harris who she was dating when

she began writing the album. *Gorgeous* may reference British actor Joe Alwyn in the way she talks about making fun of his accent and drowning in his ocean blue eyes. *Delicate* also references Joe's unusually blue eyes.

Getaway Car is most likely about actor Tom Hiddleston, with its lyrics about black ties and needing to have a reason to leave a former lover, because they met at the Met Gala Ball when she was still with Calvin. But *Delicate* and *Gorgeous*, with their allusions to blue eyes and the start of a relationship, must surely be about Joe, as they began their romance in September 2016 while the album was in production.

« & ⌄ Don Arnold/TAS18/Getty Images

Swift Insider

The fantasy drama series *Game of Thrones* inspired some of the tracks on *reputation*. *I Did Something Bad*, for instance, is based on Arya and Sansa Stark's execution of Petyr Baelish.

2019
LOVER

Swift Insider

Young musicians from the Regent Park School of Music in Toronto, Canada, perform on *It's Nice To Have A Friend* and royalties help fund low-cost lessons for disadvantaged children.

The name of the album couldn't make the content any clearer – leaving the controversy of the past years behind, this is Taylor embracing everything to do with love. The snake turns into a butterfly as seen in the video for *Me!* It's also an album with no self-doubt; it's all about taking control of life and not being a victim.

This was Taylor's first album after she left Big Machine Records. It was the time when she was asserting her rights over her own music and setting the agenda for the future.

The opening number of the Eras tour comes from this album – *Miss Americana & The Heartbreak Prince*. "This song is about disillusionment with our crazy world of politics and inequality…" Taylor says. "I wanted it to be about finding one person who really sees you and cares about you through all the noise."

Taylor highlights love and tolerance and criticises the way people spread negativity in *You Need To Calm Down*. In *The Archer* (a reference to her star sign Sagittarius) she criticises her own handling of relationships but, returning to romance, *Cornelia Street* is about the beginning of her partnership with actor Joe Alwyn that lasted longer than any of her others to date. And *London Boy* is about her return visits to Joe's home town, meeting his friends and enjoying the city.

For the video of *The Man*, Taylor played Tyler Swift with clever make-up in the video. He is an obnoxious company boss who gets away with everything because he's an alpha male. "If I had the same accomplishments, the same dating history, what would it be like if I was a man?" says Taylor.

The most poignant track about love on the album is *Soon You'll Get Better*, written when Taylor's mother was diagnosed with cancer. It has the very human lines written by a child to her parent: "And I hate to make this all about me/ But who am I supposed to talk to?/ What am I supposed to do/ If there's no you?"

« *Kevin Mazur/Getty Images* ⌃ *Brian Friedman/shutterstock. Background image: uriel/Unsplash*

2020
FOLKLORE

The *folklore* and *evermore* albums were written in the isolation of the Covid quarantine. Unable to tour as planned with the *Lover* album, she spent her time reading and watching classic movies. Their influence decided her to try a different tack and write songs that told stories from someone else's perspective instead of just her own. So three of the tracks – *cardigan*, *august* and *betty* – look at the same triangular love affair from the point of view of each of the people involved.

Others covered different subjects, as she says: "An exiled man walking the bluffs of a land that isn't his own,

wondering how it all went so terribly, terribly wrong. An embittered tormentor showing up at the funeral of his fallen object of obsession. A seventeen-year-old standing on a porch, learning to apologise."

In *epiphany* she wrote about the trauma caused by horrors seen by soldiers like her grandfather Dean in World War Two and aligned it with the trauma suffered by health workers in the pandemic. She co-wrote *exile* with boyfriend Joe Alwyn (under the pseudonym William Bowery) and he was co-producer of *illicit affairs*, *This Is Me Trying*, *August*, *My Tears Ricochet* and *Betty*.

the last great american dynasty is about eccentric Standard Oil heiress Rebekah Harkness, who owned the home Taylor

bought in Rhode Island and she contrasts that "misfit widow getting gleeful revenge on the town that cast her out" with herself. In *mad woman* she talks about powerful women being attacked and retaliating.

The album saw Taylor's first collaborations with singer/songwriter Aaron Dessner and it has a stripped-down, acoustic sound. Because they were both forced to work remotely, Dessner would send Taylor his instrumentals and she would then write the lyrics to suit.

Swift Insider

Taylor's feelings about her former boss Scott Borchetta and entrepreneur Scooter Braun, the sale of her masters and attempts to control her, are directly addressed in *mad woman*.

Kevin Mazur/TAS23/Getty Images

2020
EVERMORE

Five months after the release of *folklore* came *evermore*. In contrast to the themes of the former, which Taylor considered to be about spring and summer, *evermore* has more of an end-of-year, winter feel. One of the most emotional songs is *marjorie*, written about Taylor's opera singing grandmother in the context of regretting not doing things together before she died. As the track fades it features her grandmother's voice singing in the background, taken from some old LPs her mother owns.

Much of the album continues the trend of writing stories about other people, apart from *willow*, which is most likely about her relationship with Joe Alwyn. And in *coney island* there are cryptic clues to some of Taylor's previous relationships: Jake Gyllenhaal (Were you standing in the hallway / With a big cake, happy birthday), Calvin Harris (When I walked up to the podium I think that I forgot to say your name), Harry Styles (And when I got into the accident / The sight that flashed before me was your face), John Mayer (Did I paint your bluest skies the darkest grey?) and Tom Hiddleston (Will you forgive my soul / When you're too wise to trust me and too old to care?) *coney island* was co-written with Joe Alwyn (again credited as William Bowery), Aaron Dessner and his brother Bryce and featured their band the National on instruments and vocals.

The tracks *'tis the damn season* and *dorothea* link storylines about a woman who left her hometown for fame and fortune in Los Angeles but returns for Christmas. Her thoughts come through in the first song, while the second is from the point of view of the youthful boyfriend she left behind.

Reflecting Taylor's love of crime dramas and documentaries, *no body, no crime* is about avenging the murder of a friend when the person who did it can't be charged. And *this is me trying* is about addiction and regret for what it did to a relationship.

Swift Insider

The victim in *no body, no crime*, is called Este after one of the Haim sisters, Taylor's oftentimes backing musicians who play on that track and are also her good friends.

Kevin Winter/TAS23/Getty Images

Background image: streetsh/Unsplash

*Background image:
Jon Tyson/Unsplash*

2022
MIDNIGHTS

The quieter tones and third-person approach of *folklore* and *evermore* were left behind, along with the lower case letters, for Taylor's next album *Midnights*. When she announced its release she described it as "the stories of 13 sleepless nights scattered throughout my life" and said that it contained five main themes: self-hatred, revenge fantasies, the question of what might have been, falling in love and falling apart – the kind of things that you wake up in the dark worrying about.

The lead single from the album was *Anti-Hero*, telling the story of Tay's struggles with fame, what she hates about herself and how insecure she sometimes feels. There are a number of tracks that have been attributed to her six-year relationship with actor Joe Alwyn and Swifties have tracked the

development and eventual breakdown of the relationship through this album's tracks. *Mastermind* may refer to the beginning of their relationship when she laid a plan to date him. *Maroon* is about when they first met in New York and he was a little-known actor making his name. It also appears to allude to an early break-up that they may have got over. *Sweet Nothing* is about feeling at home with your lover and their calming presence in a tumultuous world – shades of when they got together amidst Taylor's feud with Kanye West.

Lavender Haze is about the couple coping with press intrusion, and *Glitch* definitely appears to be about him, especially in the line, "it's been two thousand one hundred ninety days of our love blackout", which is equivalent to the six years they were together.

Midnight Rain appears to outline

the conflicts in the relationship over living privately versus her career in the spotlight. These were alleged to have caused their break up a few months after the album came out, leading fans to believe that things had not been right between them for a while: "He wanted it comfortable/ I wanted that pain/ He wanted a bride/ I was making my own name/ Chasing that fame..."

Covering other relationships, *Question...?* is supposedly about the closeness she had for a while with model Karlie Kloss. *Vigilante Shit* returns to the bad associations in her life, with Scooter Braun and Kanye West, while *Karma* could be said to be a bitter track about her original mentor Scott Borchetta with lines like, "My pennies made your crown/ Trick me once, trick me twice/ Don't you know that cash ain't the only price?"

Swift Insider

In May 2022 Taylor was awarded an honorary Doctor of Fine Arts degree by New York University and in her address to the graduating class she advised them to: "Breathe in, breathe through, breathe deep and breathe out". This was the ultimate Easter Egg hint of the *Midnights* album release five months later, as *Labyrinth* contains that line.

Ronald Woan/Wikimedia Commons

2024
THE TORTURED POETS DEPARTMENT

In a surprise move, completely under everyone's radar, Taylor announced the release of a new album, *The Tortured Poets Department*, in her acceptance speech at the 2024 Grammy Awards. Fans had been expecting a Taylor's Version of the last album from the Big Machine Records days, *reputation*.

On Instagram Tay described the new album as: "An anthology of new works that reflect events, opinions and sentiments from a fleeting and fatalistic moment in time – one that was both sensational and sorrowful in equal measure." The original *TTPD* album contained 16 tracks and the subsequently released *Anthology* had another 15, making 31 tracks in total occupying just over two hours' playing time – the longest album to date.

Romance past and present of course occupy the lion's share of the tracks, with *So Long, London* clearly about the finished relationship with Joe Alwyn. *The Alchemy*, with its lines, "So when I touch down/ Call the amateurs and/ Cut 'em from the team..." is equally clearly about her new love, footballer Travis Kelce. In *So High School*, the lyrics "Are you gonna marry, kiss or kill me?" is a reference to an interview Travis gave in the course of his 2016 reality TV series *Catching Kelce* where he was asked to choose between Taylor, Katy Perry and Ariana Grande for each of the three options. In the series, 50 women – one from each US state – competed to be the one who got to date the sporting star.

Some of the album tracks muse on the ephemeral nature of fame and how you can be at the top one minute and

Kevin Mazur/TAS24/Getty Images

Kevin Mazur/TAS24/Getty Images

Rodin Eckenroth/Getty Images

Swift Insider

Spotify hosted an open-air installation at The Grove shopping centre in Los Angeles two days before the album's release. It was a library cube with shelves of books, a filing cabinet and quirky ornaments — a jar of jigsaw pieces, a tambourine, wire bird cages and lots of candlesticks.

replaced the next. *Clara Bow* reflects this at the end when the lyric says: "You look like Taylor Swift/ In this light/ We're loving it./ You've got the edge she never did./ The future's bright/ ...Dazzling."

A lot of the songs look back over her life so far, as far back as teenage years in the case of tracks such as *But Daddy I Love*

Him and *Down Bad*. And although none of them are explicit, many past relationships figure as subjects and there is more adult content in tracks such as *Guilty As Sin*.

In what is possibly a final dig at the Kanye West/Kim Kardasian clash, the styling of the track title *thanK you aIMee* spells out Kim. Although the song is ostensibly about a high school bully, it could be interpreted as Taylor saying she has come out of the feud stronger: "I built a legacy that you can't undo/ But when I count the scars, there's a moment of truth/ That there wouldn't be this if there hadn't been you." The track *Cassandra* has much more direct references to the role Kim Kardasian played in Taylor's social media cancelling.

The powerful track *Who's Afraid Of Little Old Me?* is also a hark back, this time to Tay's treatment at the hands of her original record company. It provided a dramatic live performance when she added *TTPD* to the set list on the Eras Tour, along with *Fortnight* and its undercurrents of mental health issues.

The Serious Business of Writing Songs

From the age of 12, Taylor was playing guitar and composing songs. Music came as natural to her as breathing, and she has crafted her own trail-blazing, deeply personal brand of lyrics.

⌃ *Fabio Diena/ dreamstime.com*

⌃ » **Taylor's hand-written lyrics for *Tim McGraw.*** *Ritu Manoj Jethani/ shutterstock*

» *Kevin Mazur/ TAS23/Getty Images*

Taylor's songs are poetic, unique, vulnerable but strong – reflecting a woman who knows her own mind and loves what she does. Not that she hasn't had her moments of doubt, particularly following her 'canceling' on social media in 2017, but over the years she has grown and diversified. The range of powerful songs she has been performing on her Eras Tour demonstrates this very well.

At the Nashville Songwriter Awards in 2022, in her acceptance speech for Songwriter-Artist of the decade, Taylor revealed part of her technique. She has three types of lyrics, she said, Quill, Fountain Pen, and Glitter Gel Pen. "I categorize certain songs of mine in the 'Quill' style if the words and phrasings are antiquated; if I was inspired to write

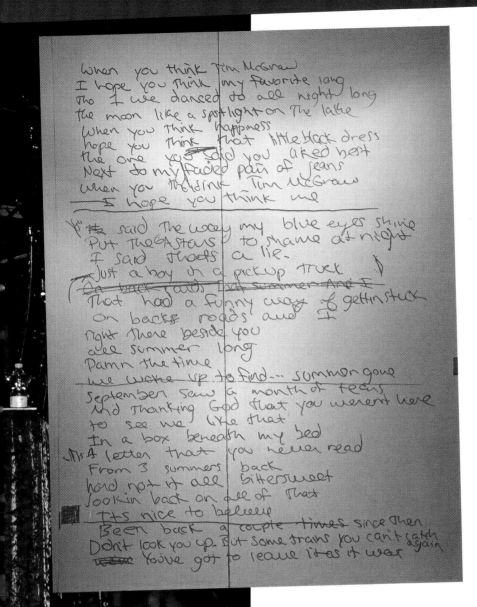

When you think Tim McGraw
I hope you think my favorite song
Tho I we danced to all night long
The moon like a spotlight on the lake
When you think happiness
hope you think that little black dress
The one you said you liked best
Next to my faded pair of jeans
When you thinking Tim McGraw
I hope you think me

Yo said the way my blue eyes shine
Put the stars to shame at night
I said that's a lie
Just a boy in a pickup truck
On back roads that summer And I
That had a funny way of gettin stuck
on backs roads and I
right there beside you
all summer long
Damn the time
we woke up to find... summer gone
September saw a month of tears
And thanking God that you weren't here
to see me like that
In a box beneath my bed
It's A letter that you never read
From 3 summers back
had not it all bittersweet
lookin back on all of that
Its nice to believe
Been back a couple times since then
Don't look you up. But some trains you can't catch again
You've got to leave it as it were

---

who tells you that you look like an angel in the bathroom. It's what we need every once in a while in these fraught times in which we live."

Songwriting has always been Taylor's strong defence mechanism. As a child it was a response to being left out of the 'in crowd' at school, as an adult it has been an answer to heartbreak and unfairness. She has always turned her bad experiences into poetry. The title of her latest album, *The Tortured Poets Department*, says it all.

"From a young age, any time I would feel pain I would think, 'It's OK, I can write about this after school,'" she says. "And still, anytime something hurts, like rejection or sadness or loneliness, or I feel joy or I fall in love, I ask myself, 'Can I write a song about this so I know how I feel?'

"I've never gotten thick skin. If you close yourself off and you get this protective armor, there is a price you pay with that - of not feeling. And feeling is important when you are a songwriter."

Swift Insider

Taylor revealed in an interview that her favourite lyrics from the *Lover* album are on the title track: "Ladies and gentlemen, will you please stand?/With every guitar string scar on my hand/I take this magnetic force of a man to be my lover."

---

it after reading Charlotte Brontë or after watching a movie where everyone is wearing poet shirts and corsets. If my lyrics sound like a letter written by Emily Dickinson's great grandmother while sewing a lace curtain, that's me writing in the Quill genre."

Fountain Pen lyrics follow a modern storyline, "with a poetic twist. Trying to paint a vivid picture of a situation, down to the chipped paint on the door frame and the incense dust on the vinyl shelf. Placing yourself and whoever is listening right there in the room where it all happened. The love, the loss, everything." She considers most of the songs she writes are Fountain Pen songs.

The last category, Glitter Gel Pen songs are her upbeat pop songs. "Glitter Gel Pen lyrics are the drunk girl at the party

"If I go more than nine days without writing a song, I get really antsy," Taylor says. "But I think the stress causes me to search my mind and helps me write. It starts with an idea that hits me at the most inconvenient time, like in the middle of a conversation or in the middle of the night, and my friends have gotten used to a glazed look coming into my eyes. Then I need to grab my phone and record a voice memo or a melody and lyrics. You never know what it will be!"

By the time she was 14, Taylor was working with experienced country music songwriter Liz Rose and had won her 'artist development' deal with RCA Records in that famous home of country music, Nashville, Tennessee. From then on she was on an unstoppable track to global superstardom. Her lyrics and music have covered such a range of styles there has always been something to resonate with the audience, whatever their age and background.

All musicians learn from, and build on, the songwriters and performers who have come before them, and Taylor is no exception. Her influences stem from a surprising array of musicians, with songs in all manner of genres. From folk to rock, hip-hop, R&B, country, classical, jazz and musical theatre – all have inspired her music and storytelling videos in one way or another.

Shoulders Of Giants

Some of her heroes' styles have been adapted as her own for a period, others she has just admired from afar. Some are household names, others best known in their own musical circles. But all have contributed a little something to the unique Taylor sound, from the vocal styling of jazz singer Ella Fitzgerald to the country twang of Shania Twain, the conversational rapping of Eminem to the stadium-filling rock anthems of Bruce Springsteen, Beyonce and Madonna. She has built on the heritage of folk singers Joni Mitchell and Bob Dylan and the heartbreak storytelling of Dolly Parton.

"I started writing songs when I was twelve and since then, it's been the compass guiding my life, and in turn, my life guided my writing. Everything I do is just an extension of my writing, whether it's directing videos or a short film, creating the visuals for a tour, or standing on stage performing. Everything is connected by my love of the craft, the thrill of working through ideas and narrowing them down and polishing it all up in the end."
—Taylor Swift

⌃ Quote from Taylor that is exhibited at the Museum of Arts and Design in New York. *Ritu Jethani/dreamstime.com*

"Getting a great idea with song writing is a lot like love. You don't know why this one is different, but it is. You don't know why this one is better, but it is. It sticks in your head, and you can't stop thinking about it."

Singer/songwriter and the band The National's frontsman, Aaron Dessner, gave an opinion echoed by many in the music business when he said: "I think Taylor is one of the greatest songwriters of all time. The poetic and literary bent of her lyricism, where songs often have elaborately woven narratives and hidden meanings that connect to her earlier or future work helps to create an entire artistic world that we all get to inhabit and obsess over as her fans."

↟ **With song-writing collaborators Ed Sheeran (left) and Jack Antonoff.** *Kevin Mazur/Getty Images*

» *Jun Sato/TAS18/ Getty Images*

Musical collaborators are important to Taylor, too, as part of her support network, and many of her close musician friends have made cameo appearances on the Eras Tour. One of her favourites is Ed Sheeran, who has not only performed and written songs with her but has been a guest in her homes and hung out with her for fun activities such as paddle boarding.

For extensive co-writing over the past few years she has chosen singer/ songwriter/music producer Jack Antonoff. They met in 2012 at the MTV Europe Music Awards, and when Jack told her he was writing something inspired by 80s band Yazoo's *Only You*, Tay said she'd like to pen the lyrics. Jack has since worked with her on individual tracks and since 2017 he has produced her new albums and the reissues of her old ones as 'Taylor's Version'.

Their partnership has benefitted them both. Taylor says: "His excitement and exuberance about writing songs is contagious. He's an absolute joy." For his part, Jack admits: "I'd been trying to produce for a while, but there was always some industry herb going, 'That's

cute, but that's not your lane'. Taylor was the first person with the stature to go, 'I like the way this sounds, I'm putting it on my album', and then, suddenly, I was allowed to be a producer."

A second major collaborator is Grammy Award-winning Aaron Dessner who worked with Tay on *folklore* and *evermore* during the Covid pandemic. She discovered Aaron was used to working remotely with his fellow The National band members because they live in different countries. "When quarantine hit and I found myself wanting to write," she says, "I reached out and he was really wanting to create too. It's been one of the most effortless collaborations and I'm very lucky to have met him."

It's a mutual appreciation. "It was as though we were just making an album for ourselves and passing time during the pandemic," he says. "It felt like we were on our own private artistic life raft, just making songs to soothe our souls and get through such an uncertain and difficult time."

« *Chen He/Visual China Group via Getty Images*

❯ *Brian Friedman/ shutterstock*

Swifties...

We would love to hear which of Tay's songs really means the most to you and why? Email *myfanstory@keypublishing.com* with SONG in the subject line and you could be in our next magazine!

How Well Do You Know Taylor's Lyrics?

In January 2024, 20-year-old Bilal Ilyas Jhandir from Pakistan set a new Guinness World Record for identifying from the first line of the lyrics, with no music, 34 Taylor Swift songs in just one minute. This broke the previous record of 27 songs held by Dan Simpson of the UK since 2019. "I have listened to each and every song of hers. I can identify almost any song of hers from the lyrics," he said. After practising for 13 weeks, he said her songs were so ingrained he was reciting them in his sleep.

So how well can you do with these pictures giving a clue to just 12 of her songs? To truly prove yourself a die-hard Swiftie like Bilal, you should name the albums they come from, too!

David Fowler/dreamstime.com

Flynt/dreamstime.com

Wikimedia Commons

Carafoto/dreamstime.com

Cammeraydave/dreamstime.com

Diego Vito Cervo/dreamstime.com

Joao Virissimo/dreamstime.com

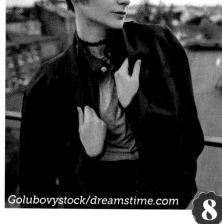

Golubovystock/dreamstime.com

Andreistanescu/dreamstime.com

Shawn Williams/dreamstime.com

Scott Aumann/dreamstime.com

ANSWERS ON PAGE 112

Marina Illarionova/dreamstime.com

A CLASS ACT

When she was a little girl, Taylor's parents arranged not only music lessons for her but also acting. So aside from her music videos, it was inevitable she would perform in film and TV roles.

Starstock/dreamstime.com

A Turn on the Silver Screen

In 2009 she appeared as herself singing her song *Crazier* at a Tennessee barn party in *Hannah Montana: The Movie* and in 2010 she won a supporting role in the film *Valentine's Day* as Felicia, a high school friend of one of the main characters. The film had a stellar cast, including Taylor's soon-to-be boyfriend, Taylor Lautner. Her song *Today Was a Fairytale* featured on the soundtrack of the film.

Two years later she was the voice of Audrey, a brave adventurer in the animated musical comedy *The Lorax* and she sang one of her unreleased songs, *Permanent Marker*. Then in 2014 she dipped a toe into science fiction films when she appeared in *The Giver* alongside movie giants Meryl Streep and Jeff Bridges. She played Rosemary, a girl who exists only as a hologram.

Taylor's childhood ambition to appear

From the director of **Pretty Woman** comes a day in the life of love.

JESSICA ALBA   KATHY BATES   JESSICA BIEL   BRADLEY COOPER
ERIC DANE   PATRICK DEMPSEY   HECTOR ELIZONDO
JAMIE FOXX   JENNIFER GARNER   TOPHER GRACE   ANNE HATHAWAY
ASHTON KUTCHER   QUEEN LATIFAH   TAYLOR LAUTNER   GEORGE LOPEZ
SHIRLEY MACLAINE   EMMA ROBERTS   JULIA ROBERTS   TAYLOR SWIFT

VALENTINE'S DAY 2.12.10

New Line Cinema

THE TRUTH LIES IN HER PAST.

THE GIVER

The Weinstein Company

in musical theatre was realised in 2019 when she took the part of Bombalurina in *Cats*. Then her next film role was in the 1930s thriller *Amsterdam* in 2022 where she was the focal point of a murder investigation.

Of course, the big film of 2023 was *The Eras Tour*, which brought the magic of a Taylor Swift concert to movie theatres and then TV screens for those not lucky enough to get a ticket for the live show.

20th Century Studios

Kevin Mazur/Getty Images

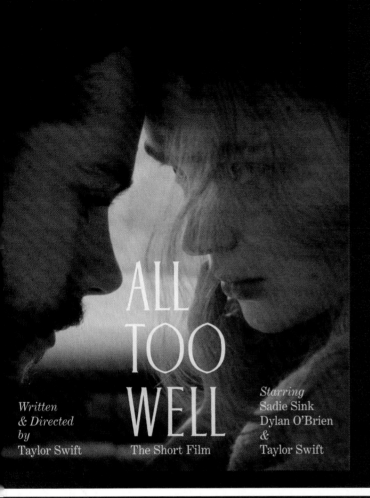

ALL TOO WELL

Written & Directed by
Taylor Swift

The Short Film

Starring
Sadie Sink
Dylan O'Brien
&
Taylor Swift

Gracing the Small Screen

Taylor's first TV role was in 2009 and was short-lived as she was a murder victim in *CSI: Crime Scene Investigation*. She had the uncomfortable job of dying in the parking lot of a motel in Las Vegas. She did get to act a bit before she got stabbed, though.

In 2013 Taylor was on TV again in a cameo role in an episode of *New Girl*, a romantic comedy about a young woman sharing a loft apartment with three single men. She played Elaine, the secret lover of an Indian man who is about to get married.

Apart from her fictional roles, Taylor made a Netflix documentary in 2020 called *Miss Americana* about her experiences in the music industry and how they have shaped her. In 2021 she wrote and directed a critically acclaimed film short based on her song *All Too Well*.

Taylor has also appeared in a number of TV adverts over the years. For Diet Coke in 2013, shoemakers Keds in 2014, telecoms company AT&T in 2017, Direct TV in 2018, Instax and Fujifilm in 2018 and Apple Music in 2019.

≈« *Taylor Swift Productions*
≈» *Coca-Cola Company/Public Domain*
« *CBS Paramount Network Television*
» *Netflix*
⌄ *20th Century Fox Television*

From Emmy® Winning Director **LANA WILSON** and
Academy Award® Winning Filmmakers Behind **20 FEET FROM STARDOM**

A NETFLIX ORIGINAL DOCUMENTARY

Miss Americana

TAYLOR SWIFT

IN SELECT THEATERS AND ON

NETFLIX | JAN 31

The people closest to Tay, colleagues and collaborators sing her praises. Even those in the music business who don't know her personally have good things to say.

What They Say About
TAYLOR

Tom Cooper/TAS23/Getty Images

Love from Family and Friends

Brother *Austin Swift*
"Something I learned myself, and learned through watching her, is respect. You just respect everyone's time, everyone that you're working with. They're all there, it's all their lives, and you need to put the work in to be worth that."

Dad *Scott Swift*
"Don't ever say never or can't do to Taylor. She started playing it four hours a day – six on the weekends." (When he suggested a 12-string guitar was too big for her small fingers.)

Mum *Andrea Swift*
"[We said] there would always be an escape hatch into normal life if she decided this wasn't something she had to pursue. But of course, that's like saying to her, 'If you want to stop breathing, that's cool.'"

Singer *Sabrina Carpenter*
"As a performer, I look up to how she's able to connect with every single person in the crowd like she's singing to them personally. And offstage she is still a superstar, but she's a superstar who's really good at baking."

Boyfriend *Travis Kelce*
"Obviously I've never dated anyone with that kind of aura about them. The scrutiny she gets… a magnifying glass on her every single day, paparazzi outside her house, outside every restaurant she goes to… And she's just living, enjoying life. When she acts like that, I better not be the one acting all strange."

Musician and friend *Alana Haim*
"She has always put her friends before herself in every situation. She's the kind of friend that checks up on us for weeks after a tough breakup and is a shoulder to lean on."

Musician and friend *Danielle Haim*
"Seeing how hard she works is insane. She never complains. She's the most incredible performer and so inspiring as a friend."

Former boyfriend *Joe Alwyn*
"[Writing with Tay] came about from messing around on a piano, and singing badly, then being overheard, and being, like, 'Let's see what happens if we get to the end of it together.' I mean, fun is such a stupid word, but it was a lot of fun."

Former boyfriend *Taylor Lautner*
"Taylor, I respect you so much. Not just for the singer you are, the songwriter, the performer, but truly for the human you are. You are gracious, humble, kind and I am honored to know you." (On stage at Eras Tour in Kansas City.)

Boyfriend's mum *Donna Kelce*
"I listened to the whole [*The Tortured Poets Department*] album, and I listened to it all morning long when it was released. I was just very impressed. She is a very talented woman, and I think it is probably her best work."

Boyfriend's father *Ed Kelce*
"She's very smart and very, very sweet, very charming, down-to-earth young woman. She's got security guys who don't want her doing anything… But if it was up to her she'd be out there with everyone who wants her."

Boyfriend's brother *Jason Kelce*
"She's the quintessential artist right now in the world. Singer-songwriter, immensely talented, an unbelievable role model for young women across the globe."

Actor and friend *Selina Gomez*
"What I love about Taylor is that she does believe in the whole love story and Prince Charming and soul mates. Because of her, I haven't lost faith."

Praise from the Music Business

Singer/songwriter Carole King

"Over the years I have known some great songwriters and I have also known some great singers and performers. It's rare to see all those talents in one person. Taylor Swift."

⌃ *Erika Goldring/FilmMagic*
« *Michael Bush/dreamstime.com*
⌄ *Jason Kempin/Getty Images*

Time *magazine's* Editor-in-Chief, Sam Jacobs

"Picking one person [to be *Time*'s Person of the Year] who represents the eight billion people on the planet is no easy task. We picked a choice that represents joy. Someone who's bringing light to the world. She was like weather, she was everywhere."

Singer/songwriter Billy Joel

"Taylor is a very talented girl and she's productive and keeps coming up with great concepts and songs and she's huge."

Country star Dolly Parton

"I think it's so important that we acknowledge the women that write and sing in country music. And I think it's also very important that they take control of their own business."

Singer/songwriter and record producer Ryan Tedder

"Taylor is the only artist that I've worked with that has the complete skillset. If she weren't an artist, she'd be the number one songwriter in the world. If she weren't a songwriter, she'd be the number one artist in the world."

Singer Jon Bon Jovi

"Taylor Swift is going to be here for as long as she chooses to be. She's growing as a person. She's growing as an artist."

⌃ *Hutchinsphoto/dreamstime.com*

The late basketball star
Kobe Bryant

"Taylor has been at the top of the game for a very, very long time. I don't care if you like her music or if you don't like her music. Look at what she's doing. It's unbelievable to be able to pull that off over and over and over."

Country songwriter
Liz Rose

"She's grown with her material and she's perfected it. She doesn't reinvent herself, she just grows. And I don't think a lot of artists can do that. They try to outsmart themselves and she's just trying to get better and evolve..."

Rock legend
Bruce Springsteen

"If you look at the music, she's an excellent writer. She is, lyrically... It's everything top 40 records should be. She is going to be a very influential artist for a long time."

Co-songwriter
Aaron Dessner

"I've spent a lot of time with her and I've never seen anyone wait on her. When I have stayed at her house, Taylor herself was cooking everyone breakfast and dinner. She's legitimately just a very down-to-earth and hardworking person."

Former boss and mentor
Scott Borchetta

"I'm always going to root for her. She's brilliant and we've had a historic run, so, yeah."

⌃ **Jack Antonoff, left, and Aaron Dessner with Taylor in 2021.** *TAS Rights Management 2021 via Getty Images*

« *Buda Mendes/TAS23/Getty Images*

The Tours

Roughly every two years since 2009 Taylor has embarked on a worldwide concert tour. Covid broke the pattern but now she's back with her most ambitious project yet, the Eras Tour.

Regular live performances are an important way for Taylor to keep in close touch with her fans. It was her ambition from a very young age to stand up in front of thousands of enthusiasts and share songs with them. "It's kind of exhilarating, walking through a crazy, insane mob. The most miraculous process is watching a song go from a tiny idea in the middle of the night to something that 55,000 people are singing back to you."

Her sell-out tours have covered many of the world's countries and venues that have been moderately sized to, increasingly these days,

huge. The curious thing is, as large as a concert space can be, and some of the stadiums she has played in have had massive capacity, her concerts still feel inclusive and personal. Sadly, though, with a packed schedule and no room for falling ill, her traditional meet and greet sessions with Swifties before and after each concert seem to have become a casualty of the Covid pandemic.

The Fearless Tour

Between April 2009 and July 2010 Taylor toured the US, Canada, England, Australia, Japan and the Bahamas with an impressive 118 shows. The

timing of the tour was to coincide with Taylor graduating from high school. To accommodate her musical commitments, she had left formal education after 10th grade and was home schooled for two years. This left room in her day for the *Fearless* album to be written, largely while she was in her Sophomore year.

Taylor was supported on tour by *American Idol* winner Kellie Pickler and country band Gloriana as well as Justin Bieber, a young 17-year-old at the beginning of his career. Special guests to join Taylor at some of the concerts included John Mayer, Faith Hill and Katy Perry.

Alexandre Paes Leme Duro/dreamstime.com

Swift Insider

When the *Fearless* tour began on April 23, 2009, in Evansville, Indiana, Taylor was presented with the key to the city and that day was declared to be Taylor Swift Day.

Bieber opened the UK leg in London where he unfortunately broke his foot on stage on the first night singing *One Time*. He did go on to finish the song, though, and open the Manchester concert.

The stage set was built with LED panels and towers in the background that were used as a backdrop for projections of images to suit each song. There was a fairytale castle in mid-stage that Tay helped design, with three winding staircases for dancers and musicians to use. The staging set the theatrical tone that would continue through all of Taylor's tours, culminating in the elaborate Eras Tour. This tour kicked off the trend for Swifties painting the number 13 on their hands (their idol's birthday), as Taylor did it for luck before each concert.

A few of the live shows were recorded to be included in a three-part mini-series called *Journey to Fearless* that was shown on children's channel The Hub in the US and came out on DVD in 2011. It is still available, although only in a Region 1 format (UK is Region 2).

The Speak Now *World Tour*

The *Speak Now* World Tour covered 13 months, four continents and 110 shows between February 2011 and March 2012. "Early on, my manager told me, 'If you want to sell 500,000 records, then go out there and meet 500,000 people.'" Well, on the *Speak Now* tour Taylor met three times that number, although not all personally! Every show was a sell-out.

As well as songs from the *Speak Now* album, Taylor included some from *Taylor Swift* and *Fearless*. As well as the painted number 13 on her right hand, during the tour she took to decorating her left arm with written out snatches of lyrics or quotes from famous films and well-known speeches.

As she made her way around North America, Taylor highlighted local artists from each city in which she performed with an acoustic cover of their songs. For instance, in Toronto she sang *You Learn* by Alanis Morissette, in Newark, New Jersey *Dancing in the Dark* by Bruce Springsteen, and in Memphis, Tennessee *Cry Me a River* by Justin Timberlake.

Most of the American continent concerts were opened by Needtobreathe, the rock band from South Carolina and in Australia it was the turn of Hot Chelle Rae from Nashville, Tennessee. In Europe and Asia she invited local artists to be her openers. Guests on this tour included Justin Bieber, Nicki Minaj, Nelly and Selena Gomez. At the Madison Square Gardens concert in New York she was joined by legendary folk-rock singer/songwriter James Taylor, after whom her parents named Taylor. Together they sang *Fire and Rain*.

Swift Insider

The title *Speak Now* is Taylor's "metaphor for so many things we go through in life; that moment where it's almost too late and you've gotta either say what it is you are feeling or deal with the consequences forever."

« Performing with
James Taylor, who
Taylor's parents
chose to name her
after. *Larry Busacca/
Getty Images*

The Red Tour

At the start of each *Red* concert between March 2013 and June 2014, Taylor arrived on stage to the rocky upbeat sounds of Lenny Kravitz's *American Woman*. It set the tone for her new style of dance, indie and Britrock sounds to emerge with the thumping beats of songs such as *Holy Ground, 22* and *We Are Never Ever Getting Back Together*. Despite the tour songs' themes of heartbreak and cheating, the mood was joyful as heard in the toe-tapping *Red* and *Mean*, which harked back to the country style.

For most of the tour the stage design was in a horseshoe shape with a catwalk in the middle of the U and a sweeping staircase. There was also a crane that lifted Taylor high above the audience while singing *Treacherous* and a larger lifting platform that raised her up for each night's surprise number. The exceptions were the shows in Asia where the stage was the conventional T shape and the lifting equipment was absent, which left *Treacherous* out of the set list.

Ed Sheeran was one of the opening acts in North America while Taylor again

selected local artists for other parts of the world. Guest appearance came from the likes of Nelly, Carly Simon, Ellie Goulding, Hunter Hayes, Jennifer Lopez and Sara Bareilles.

The tour had been scheduled for a concert in Bangkok, Thailand, in June 2014, on the Southeast Asian leg. But two weeks before, the Royal Thai Army mounted a coup d'etat and overthrew the current government, martial law was imposed and a curfew was in place. The promoters had safety concerns about a concert that would bring a large number of people together and so they cancelled. Taylor turned to social media to tell her Thai fans how sorry she was that she could not perform for them.

Swift Insider

Club Red, the room set aside at each venue on the tour for some lucky Swifties to hang out with Taylor after the show, had red and grey themed furnishings, red lighting, soft drinks available in cooler buckets and jelly bean dispensing machines.

Swift Insider

On this tour, for the first time, each fan was given an LED bracelet as they entered the venue that was controlled by the production crew and turned the audience into part of the show's lighting effects.

The 1989 *World Tour*

The *1989* tour marked Taylor's complete departure from country music when it ran from May to December 2015. Although there were only 85 shows, as opposed to the *Fearless* tour's 110, audiences had grown by a million thanks to the venues being larger – stadiums, arenas and sports grounds rather than concert halls.

Australian Vance Joy was the opening act for all the concerts apart from the three in Germany and the Netherlands when the UK's James Bay led the way. A number of the models, singers and actors who the media were by now referring to as Taylor's 'Squad' made guest appearances – Cara Delevingne, Selena Gomez, Gig Hadid, Lena Dunham, Karlie Kloss and Heidi Klum were just some of them. The legendary Joan Baez joined her for the Santa Clara, California concert and Mick Jagger sang *(I Can't Get no) Satisfaction* with her at one of the Nashville gigs.

And the list of A-listers went on, with Julia Roberts, Matt LeBlanc, Alison Krauss, Miranda Lambert, Ed Sheeran, Dixie Chicks, Wiz Khalifa, Justin Timberlake, Avril Lavigne, Lorde, Chris Rock and Ricky Martin among many others, all making an appearance. Taylor explained in an interview why there were so many from all walks of showbusiness and sporting life. "In this generation, I know as I'm walking on stage that a huge percentage of the crowd have already YouTubed the entire show and watched the whole thing online. They know the set list, they know the costumes, they've looked it up. That presented me with an interesting issue. I love the element of surprise... so going into this tour, [I arranged] having people pop on stage that you didn't expect to see."

Singer John Legend was not scheduled to be a special guest, but Taylor had a text from her friend, John's wife, saying they were at the Los Angeles show. Allowing the band only 35 minutes to learn the song, she persuaded Legend to sing *All Of Me* with her.

After the last show of the tour a full concert movie, *The 1989 World Tour LIVE*, was released featuring concert footage, interviews, backstage scenes and rehearsals.

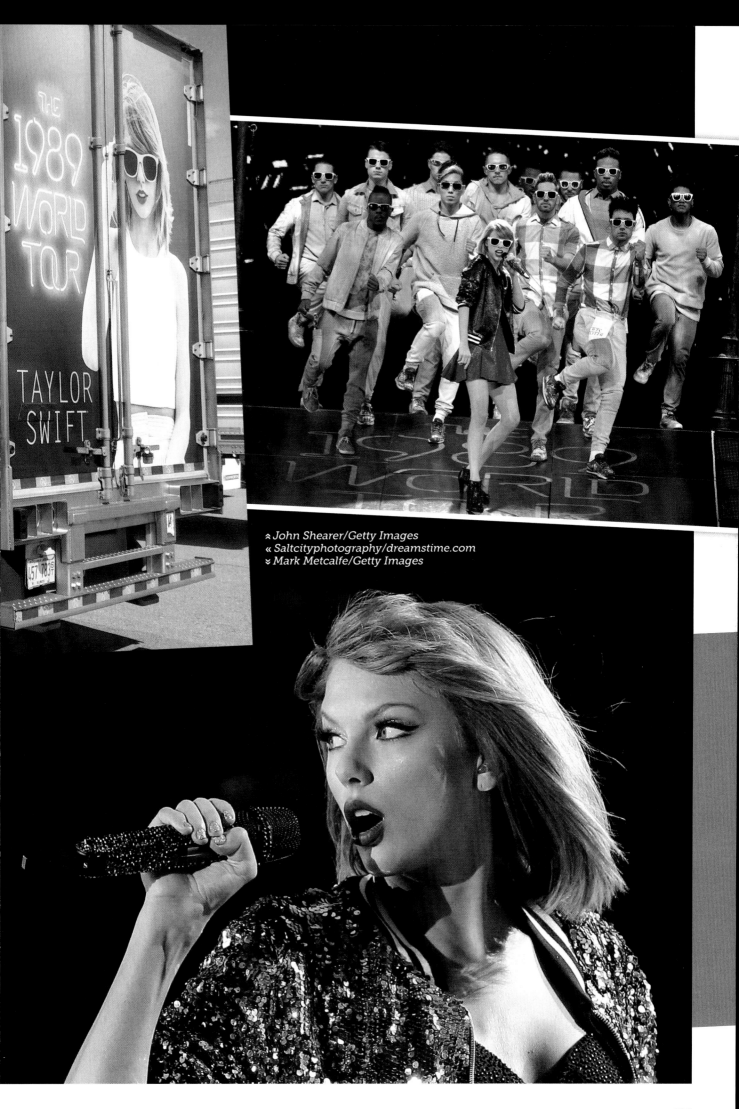

≫ John Shearer/Getty Images
« Saltcityphotography/dreamstime.com
≫ Mark Metcalfe/Getty Images

The reputation Stadium Tour

The *reputation* tour began in May 2018 and ended that November. It consisted of just 53 concerts visiting only seven countries but it was her biggest yet in terms of earnings and number of people attending as all the concerts were held in giant venues.

The tour followed a long period during which Taylor withdrew from most high-profile events and social media as a result of her long-running feud with Kanye West and Kim Kardashian that had culminated in Kardashian calling her 'a snake'. The staging for the tour leaned heavily on this insult with snakes appearing all over the place as set decorations and costume details. During the song *Look What You Made Me Do*, pointedly calling out the people who had tried to damage Taylor's reputation, a giant inflatable snake arrived on stage.

The stage itself had two runways radiating left and right from the centre and two satellite stages in the middle of the arena with more giant snakes curving up their lighting rigs. These extra stages were accessed via a floating gondola. During the Philadelphia concert the gondola broke down and Taylor

⌃ *Christian Bertrand/ shutterstock*
» *Jun Sato/TAS18/ Getty Images*
» » *Jun Sato/TAS18/ Getty Images*
» » ⌄ *Ronald Woan/Wikimedia Commons*
⌄ *Chbm89/ dreamstime.com*

Swift Insider

Taylor designed the stage to have a quick changing area for her to exchange costumes eight times. It looks like it was a practice session for the 16 costume changes on the Eras Tour!

couldn't reach the second stage and had to perform all the planned numbers on the third stage. The band was hidden behind the main projection screen, which occasionally opened to reveal them playing.

The opening act was shared between Camila Cabello and Charli XCX and this time round there were fewer surprise guests, only appearing in 10 of the concerts. But they did include Robbie Williams, Bryan Adams, Tim McGraw and Faith Hill, Shawn Mendes and Selena Gomez.

Connecting with the fans was the important thing for Taylor on this tour, hence the staging that she devised to give the maximum number of fans on the arena floor the chance to get close. As she said: "I learned that I have friends and fans in my life who don't care if I'm #canceled. They were there in the worst times and they're here now. The fans and their care for me, my well-being, and my music were the ones who pulled me through. The most emotional part of the *reputation* Stadium Tour for me was knowing I was looking out at the faces of the people who helped me get back up. I'll never forget the ones who stuck around."

The Eras Tour

All Taylor's tours to date had been promotions for a single album, with just occasional older songs thrown in. The Eras Tour between March 2023 and December 2024 was her most ambitious concept yet and designed to introduce all her albums and their new *Taylor's Versions*.

The set designs had to be correspondingly ambitious and have proved to be spectacular. The three-hour journey starts the audience in the cotton candy pink, billowing parachute silks of the opening *Lover* numbers, passing through a giant dolls house and high-rise city office to the golden glow of *Fearless*. The come the crimson tones of *Red,* the flower-filled pastures of the *Speak Now* era, the scarlet and black, snakes and candles of *reputation,* and the log cabin and fairytale forest of the *folklore* era. This transitions into the dark woods of *evermore* with its giant trees and on to the AC Cobra car taking a golf club beating in the *1989* section. Since the European leg of the tour started, an impressive spaceship and stark hospital room have been added to represent *The Tortured Poets Department* era and the concert culminates in the darkness of the closing numbers from *Midnights.*

⌃ Kevin Mazur/TAS24/Getty Images
» Ronald Woan/Wikimedia Commons
»⌄ Kevin Mazur/TAS24/Getty Images
⌄ Buda Mendes/TAS23/Getty Images

Dressing Up the Eras

An array of costumes appropriate to the leading themes of each era have also been created by the world's top designers:

Fausto Puglisi/Roberto Cavalli (*reputation* snake outfit, *Fearless* fringed mini dress, *1989* beaded and sequinned mini skirts and bustiers, chiffon dresses for the acoustic numbers)

Donatella Versace (*Lover* bodysuits and blazers)

Nicole + Felicia (*Speak Now* gowns)

Elie Saab (*Speak Now* dresses)

Zuhair Murad (*Speak Now* gowns and *Midnights* body suit and garter)

Ashish Gupta (*Red* sequinned slogan T-shirt, coat dress and body suit)

Alberta Ferretti (*folklore* gowns)

Etro custom-made (*evermore* dresses)

Oscar de la Renta (*Midnights* bodysuits, mini dress and lavender fur coat)

Vivienne Westwood (*The Tortured Poets Department* outfits)

Christian Louboutin knee-high and ankle boots with signature red soles

≪ Buda Mendes/TAS23/Getty Images
≫ Kevin Mazur/TAS24/Getty Images

Swift Insider

Between the last acoustic number and the *Midnights* section, Taylor dives into a hole that opens at the end of the long catwalk. It then looks and sounds like she's underwater, swimming back to the main stage. In fact, she lands on a padded sled on rails below the stage that zips her back under the catwalk.

Swifties...

Have you been to a Taylor concert?
We would love to hear your experience
of the magic and see your selfies!
Email *myfanstory@keypublishing.com*
with TOUR in the Subject line and you
could be in our next magazine!

⌃ *Ashok Kumar/TAS24/Getty Images*
⌄ *Paolo V via Wikimedia Commons*

Ringing the Changes

« & ⌃ **The old and new *Lover* bodysuit.** *Andres Dias Nobre/AFP; Julien de Rosa/AFP via Getty*

When the Eras show came to Europe in May 2024, Taylor added in songs from The Tortured Poets Department. *In line with her love of surprises, she also made some costume changes.*

The Tortured Poets Department album had only been released nine months into the tour and the extended Christmas break gave the team time to rehearse the seven new songs and the set builders to create a spectacle with new staging.

Apart from the *Tortured Poets* costumes, all created by designer Vivienne Westwood, there were colour changes for the *Lover* body suits, and the Versace jacket Taylor wears to sing *The Man*. The *1989* crop top and flared mini skirt got new colourways, as did the flounced dress for the acoustic section and the gowns for *folklore/evermore*. Her *Fearless* fringed dress took on a look that was similar to the one she wore for the original *Fearless* tour in 2009 and the *Red* sequinned T-shirt got a new slogan: "This is not Taylor's Version".

To make room for the new numbers, several of the original ones were dropped and the *folklore* and *evermore* sections were merged. Gone were *The Archer, Long Live, invisible string, tolerate it, the last great american dynasty, no body, no crime, the 1* and *'tis the damn season.* Fresh in were *But Daddy I Love Him, So High School, Who's Afraid of Little Old Me?, Down Bad, Fortnight, The Smallest Man Who Ever Lived* and *I Can Do it With a Broken Heart.*

There was also a change in the running order of the eras. *Lover* and *Fearless* still led the way but then *Red* and *evermore* swapped places when the latter joined in the *folklore* section. The new *Tortured Poets* section was inserted between *1989* and the acoustic section. *Midnights* retained its position as the finale.

« & ⌄ One of the original and the new colourway for *The Man*. *Suzanne Cordeiro/AFP via Getty; Julien de Rosa/AFP via Getty*

« & ⌃ The old and new *Fearless* dresses and (left) the 2009 original the new look emulates. *Scott Eisen/TAS23/ Getty Images; Kevin Mazur/ TAS24/Getty Images; Everett Collection/ shutterstock*

˅ & » The colour change for the *1989* era. *Pedro Gomes/TAS24/Getty Images; Kevin Mazur/ TAS24/Getty Images*

˅ & » The original colour for the acoustic number dress and the new blue version. *Both Kevin Mazur/Getty Images*

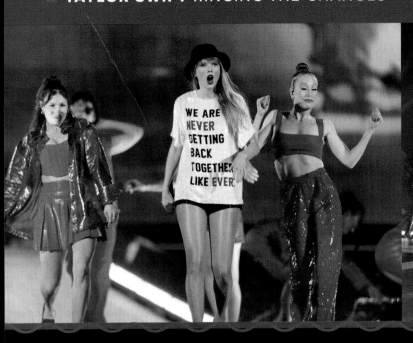

« & ⌄ Taylor had a new slogan for the *Red* era. *Omar Vega/ TAS23/Getty Images; Kevin Mazur/TAS24/Getty Images*

The introduced yellow *folklore* gown.
Kevin Mazur/Getty Images

Eras on Display

Following Taylor's first hugely successful concert dates in the UK capital in June, the famous Victoria & Albert Museum in South Kensington, London, created a new exhibition to showcase her eras. From July 27th to September 8th it was free for visitors to take the Taylor Swift Songbook Trail through the museum's galleries to see a celebration of her lyrics and music videos. Each one of the 13 stops on the trail shone a light on costumes worn on tour or in film, along with some of her music awards, storyboards for her videos and musical instruments.

A similar exhibition occupied The Museum of the Arts and Design in New York at the end of 2023, entitled Taylor Swift: Storyteller. And, at the same time as the V&A display went on show, the small local museum at Stone Harbor, in New Jersey, where a young Taylor and her family spent many happy holidays, opened a showcase of her memorabilia including childhood photographs lent by her parents.

The gown for *The Tortured Poets Department* was made of recycled taffeta and decorated with hand-written text reading: "I love you, it's ruining my life", from the song *Fortnight*. *Kevin Mazur/ TAS24/Getty Images*

The white gown was worn over a white, black or gold bikini and was removed on stage and replaced by a tailcoat in the *I Can Do It With a Broken Heart* number. *Kevin Mazur/ TAS24/Getty Images*

Top Tour
Stats

Taylor's tours are packed full of greatest and highest figures and fascinating statistics

Gross earnings from each tour

Fearless	$66,500,000
Speak Now	$123,700,000
Red	$150,200,000
1989	$250,700,000
Reputation	$345,700,000
Eras (up to Dec 2023)	$1,039,263,762

Number of attendees

Fearless	1,200,000
Speak Now	1,640,000
Red	1,700,000
1989	2,280,000
Reputation	2,939,000
Eras (up to Dec 2023)	4,350,000

Speak Now Tour

Highest grossing tour by a female artist

1989 Tour

Chosen one of *Rolling Stone* magazine's 50 Greatest Concerts of the Last 50 Years

Number of shows

Fearless	118
Speak Now	110
Red	86
1989	85
Reputation	53
Eras	152

$2 BILLION

Eras Tour first concert tour to take $2 billion at the box office

Number of countries

Fearless	6
Speak Now	19
Red	12
1989	11
Reputation	7
Eras	22

reputation Tour

Won Top Tour, Tour of the Year and Best Pop Tour from the American Music Awards, Billboard magazine's Touring Awards, the People's Choice and Teen Choice Awards, iHeartRadio Music Awards and Pollstar magazine awards

Countries visited on every tour

USA
Canada
England
Japan
Australia

Red Tour

Taylor's last tour billed as a country artist

ONE MINUTE

Fearless Tour

Tickets for New York's Madison Square Gardens concert sold out in a record one minute

Countries visited on only one tour

The Bahamas	(Fearless)
South Korea	(Speak Now)
Hong Kong	(Speak Now)
Belgium	(Speak Now)
Norway	(Speak Now)
Northern Ireland	(Speak Now)
Indonesia	(Red)
Malaysia	(Red)
Mexico	(Eras)
Argentina	(Eras)
Brazil	(Eras)
Sweden	(Eras)
Portugal	(Eras)
Wales	(Eras)
Switzerland	(Eras)
Poland	(Eras)
Austria	(Eras)

@EKELLEYDESIGN

IN M
Phi
ER
MAY 12-14,
WELCOME HOMI
Q102 PHILLY

Painting the Town...

Taylor

The UK concerts on the Eras Tour inspired new outdoor murals in Liverpool and London – the latest in a host of amazing street art around the world celebrating Taylor's music.

I t began in May 2023, when 27-year-old artist, TikToker and ardent Swiftie Emily Kelley began a social media quest to persuade the US city of Philadelphia to do something to celebrate the Eras Tour coming to their town. During the Covid pandemic art college graduate Emily filled in her quarantine time by creating Swift-inspired artworks that she sells online at www.ekelleydesign.com so she was used to drawing her heroine.

Being such a fan, and knowing Taylor had been born an hour away from the Lincoln Financial Field arena in Philly where she was performing, Emily proposed painting a mural if someone would donate the use of a wall. "Philly is such a city full of public art that this just makes sense to welcome her home," she told online local news source phillyvoice.com. "And it's something that no other city has done before."

Eventually, radio station Q102 commissioned the artwork on the boarded-up windows of a building that was up for rent at 207 South Street, Philadelphia and Emily began to plan the 4.25m x 2m painting. "I was not confident

A vibrant pink Taylor Swift mural in Sydney, Australia. *Catrina Haze/ shutterstock*

in my ability to sketch something on such a big surface. You know, the portrait of Taylor is just as tall as I am and I've never done anything to that scale. But I'm really glad to say it did work.

"I wanted to include a bunch of little icons or something that had to do with Taylor that maybe you wouldn't know unless you were a fan." Emily drafted in other young artists to help her paint it, having drawn the outline of the design on the wall.

The Philadelphia mural that started the trend. *Emily Kelley*

International craze

The trend for outdoor artworks of Taylor continued when the Eras Tour moved on to Mexico. Local street artist Pincelarte chose her *1989* era for his tribute on the wall of his house in Veracruz.

Across the other side of the world, in Australia, on the corner of William and Crown Streets in Sydney, artist Catrina Haze pictured Taylor as she was in her *Lover* era in the

outfit she wore to the 2019 MTV Video Music Awards. Meanwhile, just north of Sydney in Crows Nest, New South Wales, Manny's Music Store in Alexander Street commissioned aerosol artist Sidney Tapia to spray a mural of Tay in black and white backed by a starburst of colour.

Then, later in the tour, the UK went Taylor artwork mad in Liverpool and London…

⌃Pincelarte's portrait in Veracruz, Mexico. *@pincelartemx/Instagram*
«**Emily and one of the young artists at work on the mural.** *Emily Kelley*

Liverpool's Phoenix Hotel decorated with pictures of Taylor's eras.
MurWalls.com/Tiktok

Liverpool gave Swifties a great Scouser welcome by renaming the city Taylor Town and creating a Taylor Swift trail of artworks for them to follow. There were 11 art installations, each one inspired by one of Tay Tay's albums. The wall art part of the trail was painted on New Bird Street by Molly Mural, influenced by the *Fearless* era and Taylor's lucky number 13. On her website, artist Molly Hawkins said: "Creating this mural was an exciting challenge that allowed me to blend vibrant aesthetics with a sense of community and celebration. I'm thrilled to have been part of this project, showcasing the incredible spirit of Liverpool and the global phenomenon that is Taylor Swift."

In another part of Liverpool, street art company MurWalls (www.MurWalls.com) installed a portrait from the opening numbers of the tour with a background of illustrations depicting each of Taylor's eras in different coloured panels. It was found on a familiar site for murals in the city, beside the Phoenix Hotel in Foley Street, two miles from the city centre. As the hotel is close to Anfield Stadium, where the Eras concerts were being held, it was front and centre for passing fans.

One of MurWalls' artists, Humor, was responsible for their second Taylor mural, a giant four-panel headshot behind the Spanish Steps at Wembley Stadium in London, location of Taylor's London concerts. This time, the portrait was surrounded by song lyrics from every era, with the exception of *folklore*. The words came from *Teardrops On My Guitar, Fearless, Long Live, Starlight, Out Of The Woods, Getaway Car, Lover, Champagne Problems, You're On Your Own Kid*, and *But Daddy I Love Him*.

Round the corner was a different type of street art from spray painter Frank Styles, who created a 2.4m image of Taylor split into strips, each of which was attached to the riser of

⌃ Taylor's image spreading up the Wembley steps, renamed Swiftie Steps for the occasion. *Catriona Branch*
⌃» The MurWalls street art by Humor at Wembley Stadium. *Catriona Branch*

the steps that connect Wembley Stadium to Wembley Arena. Together they made a full portrait when viewed from a distance. Frank, who comes from the northeast of England, appealed on social media for the loan of a blank wall, which a local garage was happy to supply. The resulting work was photographed and then printed onto panels of vinyl that could be stuck to the backs of the steps. Around Taylor's face are Easter Eggs for Swifties to work out, referring to songs including *Red, Our Song, 22, Look What You Made Me Do* and *Fearless*.

Swifties...

Have you got a Taylor mural near you? We'd love to see your selfies with it! Email myfanstory@keypublishing.com with MURAL in the subject line and your picture could be in our next magazine!

Molly Mural's brightly painted collection of images reflecting Taylor's Fearless album. *Daniel Lezano*

Wise Words

Apart from her amazing, inciteful song lyrics, Taylor has come up with some great quotes about life in general.

"Being sweet to everyone all the time can get you into a lot of trouble... can contribute to some of your life's worst regrets if someone takes advantage of this trait in you. Grow a backbone, trust your gut, and know when to strike back. Be like a snake – only bite if someone steps on you."

"Trying and failing and trying again and failing again is normal. It's good to mess up and learn from it and take risks."

"Social media can be great, but it can also inundate your brain with images of what you aren't, how you're failing, or who is in a cooler locale than you at any given moment. One thing I do to lessen this weird insecurity laser beam is to turn off Comments."

"Words can break someone into a million pieces, but they can also put them back together. I hope you use yours for good, because the only words you'll regret more than the ones left unsaid are the ones you use to intentionally hurt someone."

"Just be yourself... there is no one better."

"I learned to stop hating every ounce of fat on my body. I worked hard to retrain my brain that a little extra weight means curves, shinier hair, and more energy. I think a lot of us push the boundaries of dieting but taking it too far can be really dangerous. There is no quick fix. I work on accepting my body every day."

"Life isn't how to survive the storm, it's about how to dance in the rain."

"Before you jump in headfirst, maybe, I don't know... get to know someone! All that glitters isn't gold, and first impressions actually aren't everything."

"Every day I try to remind myself of the good in the world, the love I've witnessed and the faith I have in humanity. We have to live bravely in order to truly feel alive, and that means not being ruled by our greatest fears."

"The lesson I've learned the most often in life is that you're always going to know more in the future than you know now."

"Learning the difference between lifelong friendships and situationships. It's sad but sometimes when you grow, you outgrow relationships. You may leave behind friendships along the way, but you'll always keep the memories."

"Every part of you that you've ever been, every phase you've ever gone through, was you working it out in that moment with the information you had available to you at the time. There's a lot that I look back at like, 'Wow, a couple of years ago I might have cringed at this.' You should celebrate who you are now, where you're going, and where you've been."

Bob Levey/
TAS23/Getty
Images

Mat Hayward/TAS23/Getty Images

"You can draw inspiration from anything. If you're a good storyteller, you can take a dirty look somebody gives you, or if a guy you used to have flirtations with starts dating a new girl, or somebody you're casually talking to says something that makes you so mad – you can create an entire scenario around that."

"Unique and different is the new generation of beautiful. You don't have to be like everyone else."

"There might be times when you put your whole heart and soul into something, and it is met with cynicism or scepticism, but you can't let that crush you. You have to let that fuel you, because we live in a world where anyone has the right to say anything that they want about you at any time, but just please remember that you have the right to prove them wrong."

"No matter what happens in life, be good to people. Being good to people is a wonderful legacy to leave behind."

"In fairy tales you meet Prince Charming and he's everything you ever wanted. In fairy tales the bad guy is very easy to spot. The bad guy is always wearing a black cape so you always know who he is. Then you grow up and you realize that Prince Charming is not as easy to find as you thought. You realize the bad guy is not wearing a black cape and he's not easy to spot; he's really funny, and he makes you laugh, and he has perfect hair."

"I've learned that disarming someone's petty bullying can be as simple as learning to laugh."

"It's so much easier to like people, and to let people in, to trust them until they prove that you should do otherwise. The alternative is being an iceberg."

"Silence speaks so much louder than screaming tantrums. Never give anyone an excuse to say that you're crazy."

"It's impressive when someone can charm people instantly and own the room, but what I know now to be more valuable about a person is not their charming routine upon meeting them (I call it a "solid first 15"), but the layers of a person you discover in time."

"One element of Madonna's career that really takes center stage is how many times she's reinvented herself. It's easier to stay in one look, one comfort zone, one musical style. It's inspiring to see someone whose only predictable quality is being unpredictable."

"Real life is a funny thing, you know. In real life, saying the right thing at the right moment is beyond crucial. So crucial, in fact, that most of us start to hesitate, for fear of saying the wrong thing at the wrong time. But lately what I've begun to fear more that that is letting the moment pass without saying anything. I think most of us fear reaching the end of our life, and looking back, regretting the moments we didn't speak up. When we didn't say 'I love you'. When we should've said 'I'm sorry'. When we didn't stand up for ourselves or someone who needed help."

"I make countdowns for things I'm excited about. When I've gone through dark, low times, I've always found a tiny bit of relief and hope in getting a countdown app (they're free) and adding things I'm looking forward to. Even if they're not big holidays or anything, it's good to look toward the future. Sometimes we can get overwhelmed in the now, and it's good to get some perspective that life will always go on, to better things."

"I've learned that society is constantly sending very loud messages to women that exhibiting the physical signs of aging is the worst thing that can happen to us. These messages tell women that we aren't allowed to age. It's an impossible standard to meet... telling women we're supposed to defy gravity, time, and everything natural in order to achieve this bizarre goal of everlasting youth that isn't even remotely required of men."

"Anything you put your mind to and add your imagination into can make your life a lot better and a lot more fun."

"If you can wind the tension of an argument down to a conversation about where the other person is coming from, there's a greater chance you can remove the shame of losing a fight for one of you and the ego boost of the one who 'won' the fight."

On to the f

For 2024 the show goes on – a feast of visuals and the pleasure of Taylor's music spanning her 18 years of recording. But come December the whole Eras phenomenon will be over, so what comes next? Almost certainly a *reputation* (*Taylor's Version*) album and, based on her touring life so far, Taylor will undoubtedly have been writing songs as she travelled the world. A year in the studio and then, maybe, a brand-new album in 2026? That will definitely be something to look forward to but, knowing Taylor's love of surprises, there's bound to be something else before then that none of us were expecting!

» *Bob Levey/TAS23/Getty Images*

uture...

"When I'm 40 and nobody wants to see me in a sparkly dress anymore, I'll be, like: 'Cool, I'll just go in the studio and write songs for kids.' It's looking like a good pension plan."

Quiz Answers

How well have you done?

> 66 Now it's like snow at the beach, weird, but f*****' beautiful... 99

Snow on the Beach
from *Midnights*

1

2

> 66 A message in a bottle is all I can do, standin' here, hoping it gets to you... 99

Message in a Bottle
from *Red (Taylor's Version)*

3

> 66 We'll move to an island and he can be my jailer, Burton to this Taylor... 99

Ready For It?
from *reputation*

> 66 And I don't know why, but with you I'd dance in a storm in my best dress. 99

Fearless from *Fearless (Taylor's Version)*

4

6

5

> 66 Roaring twenties, tossing pennies in the pool, and if my wishes came true it would've been you. 99

the 1 from *folklore*

> 66 Do you remember, we were sittin' there by the water? You put your arm around me for the first time. 99

Mine from *Speak Now (Taylor's Version)*

8

> 66 I, I, I shake it off, I shake it off (ooh). 99

Shake It Off
from *1989 (Taylor's Version)*

7

> 66 Windows flung right open, autumn air, jacket 'round my shoulders is yours. 99

Cornelia Street
from *Lover*

Background images: Nechama Lock/Olga Thelavart/Unsplash

9

❝ It only feels this raw right now, lost in the labyrinth of my mind. ❞

Labyrinth
from *Midnights*

❝ Life was a willow and it bent right to your wind. ❞

willow
from *evermore*

10

11

❝ You're not Dylan Thomas, I'm not Patti Smith, this ain't the Chelsea Hotel, we're modern idiots. ❞

The Tortured Poets Department
from *The Tortured Poets Department: The Anthology*

❝ He's the reason for the teardrops on my guitar, the only thing that keeps me wishin' on a wishing star. ❞

Teardrops on my Guitar
from *Taylor Swift*

12

Ashok Kumar/TAS24/Getty Images

Win!

Your chance to own ALL FIVE special/limited edition Taylor Swift *The Tortured Poets Department* vinyls!

How would you like to have all five versions of Taylor Swift's *The Tortured Poets Department* vinyls in your collection? Our easy to enter competition gives you the chance to own not only the clear and white LPs, but also all three special editions featuring three exclusive tracks! Our prize bundle includes the following:

- Special Edition vinyl + bonus track - '*The Black Dog*'
- Special Edition vinyl + bonus track - '*The Bolter*'
- Special Edition vinyl + bonus track - '*The Albatross*'
- Limited Edition Phantom Clear vinyl
- Limited Edition Ghosted White vinyl

Winning this amazing prize couldn't be easier – all you have to do is scan the QR code with your smartphone (or type the url into your web browser), fill in your details, and that's it – you're in with a chance of winning this amazing prize! Closing date for entries is January 31, 2025.

Scan with your phone to enter

If you can't use our QR code don't worry, you can still enter by typing the following into your web browser:

https://shop.keypublishing.com/pages/win-tortured-poets-vinyls